English as a global language
Second edition

David Crystal, world authority on the English language, presents a lively and factual account of the rise of English as a global language and explores the whys and wherefores of the history, current status and future potential of English as the international language of communication. English has been lauded as the most 'successful' language ever, with 1,500 million speakers worldwide; but Crystal avoids taking sides and tells the story in a measured but engaging way, backed by facts and figures. This new edition of his classic book contains extra sections (on subjects including the linguistic features of New Englishes, the future of English as a world language, and the possibility of an English 'family' of languages), footnotes and a full bibliography. There are updates throughout. This is a book for anyone of any nationality concerned with English: teachers, students, language professionals, politicians, general readers and anyone with a love of the language.

DAVID CRYSTAL is one of the world's foremost authorities on language. He is author of the hugely successful *Cambridge encyclopedia of language* (1987; second edition 1997), *Cambridge encyclopedia of the English language* (1995), *Language death* (2000), *Language and the Internet* (2001) and *Shakespeare's words* (2002, with Ben Crystal). An internationally renowned writer, journal editor, lecturer and broadcaster, he received an OBE in 1995 for his services to the study and teaching of the English language. His edited books include several editions of *The Cambridge encyclopedia* (1990–2000) and related publications, *Words on words* (2000, with Hilary Crystal) and *The new Penguin encyclopedia* (2002).

English as a global language

Second edition

DAVID CRYSTAL

2003

CAMBRIDGE
UNIVERSITY PRESS

PUBLISHED BY THE PRESS SYNDICATE OF THE UNIVERSITY OF CAMBRIDGE
The Pitt Building, Trumpington Street, Cambridge CB2 1RP, United Kingdom

CAMBRIDGE UNIVERSITY PRESS
The Edinburgh Building, Cambridge, CB2 2RU, UK
40 West 20th Street, New York, NY 10011-4211, USA
477 Williamstown Road, Port Melbourne, VIC 3207, Australia
Ruiz de Alarcón 13, 28014 Madrid, Spain
Dock House, The Waterfront, Cape Town 8001, South Africa

http://www.cambridge.org

First published 1997
Second edition 2003
Reprinted 2004

Printed in the United Kingdom at the University Press, Cambridge

Typefaces Galliard 10.5/13 pt and Formata   *System* LaTeX 2$_\varepsilon$ [TB]

A catalogue record for this book is available from the British Library

ISBN 0 521 82347 1 hardback
ISBN 0 521 53032 6 paperback

Contents

111132

Contents

List of tables

Preface to the second edition

Although *English as a global language* did not appear until 1997, it was actually written in 1995, which in 2002 seems a very long time ago, as far as global linguistic developments are concerned. The 1990s were a revolutionary decade, in that respect, with a proliferation of new linguistic varieties arising out of the worldwide implementation of the Internet, an emerging awareness of the crisis affecting the world's endangered languages, and an increasingly public recognition of the global position of English. Academic publications relating to this last topic seriously increased in number and weight. The largely article-driven literature of previous decades had typically been exploratory and programmatic, restricted to individual situations, anecdotal in illustration, lacking a sociolinguistic frame of reference, and focusing on the written (and usually literary) language. By contrast, the 1990s saw the emergence of a more comprehensive perspective in which spoken varieties became prominent, there was a real increase in the amount of descriptive data, and attempts were made to arrive at explanations and to make predictions of an appropriately general and sociolinguistically informed character.

In particular, several book-length treatments of English appeared, each providing a personal synthesis of previous observations and speculations, and focusing on the phenomenon of global English as an end in itself. By the end of the decade, the different attitudes had highlit a number of important theoretical issues, and made it possible to see the various kinds of focus adopted by individual authors. I came to see the first edition of the present book, as a consequence, more clearly as predominantly a retrospective account, examining the range of historical factors which have led to the current position of English in the world. Although avoiding firm predictions about the future, I thought it likely that English 'has already grown to be independent of any form of social control' (1st edition, p. 139). In my view the momentum of growth has become so great that there is nothing likely to stop its continued spread as a global lingua franca, at least in the foreseeable future. Other books took different perspectives. For example, David Graddol's *The future of English*, published in 1998, looked towards the future, beginning with the present-day situation, and examining the contemporary trends likely to affect the language's eventual role. For him, English is certainly stoppable. Emphasizing the unpredictability inherent in language use, he suggested that 'the current global wave of English may lose momentum' (p. 60) and saw the real possibility of new language hierarchies emerging in the next century, with English holding a less global position. Then Tom McArthur, in *The English languages*, also published in 1998, adopted a more synchronic perspective, moving away from a monolithic concept of English. His primary focus was on the kinds of variation encountered in the language as a consequence of its global spread. He suggested that English was undergoing a process of radical change which would eventually lead to fragmentation into a 'family of languages'.

The role of these books has been to underline some of the parameters of inquiry which must influence the next wave of empirical studies. From a stage when there were few general hypotheses to motivate research, we now have a multiplicity of them. Some are issues relating to language use: several political, economic, demographic and social factors have been identified as potential influences on world language presence, all of which have been recognized as operating at local regional levels, such as in relation to minority languages or endangered languages; however, the role of such factors at a global level remains virtually unexplored. Others are issues affecting language structure: the way in which regional and social factors influence the growth of language varieties and foster linguistic change has formed much of the subject-matter of sociolinguistics and dialectology; but here, too, there is as yet little understanding of what happens when these processes begin to operate at a macro level. To take just one example: the radical diversification envisioned by McArthur could have several outcomes, certainly including the development of an English family of languages, but also resulting in various forms of multiglossia (going well beyond current conceptions of diglossia), the emergence of more complex notions of 'standard', and different kinds of multidialectism. We have as yet no adequate typology of the remarkable range of language contact situations which have emerged as a consequence of globalization, either physically (e.g. through population movement and economic development) or virtually (e.g. through Internet communication and satellite broadcasting).

I originally wrote *English as a global language* as (what I hoped would be) a straightforward read, and chose not to impede the flow for a general reader by providing an array of academic footnotes and a full bibliographical apparatus. When I wanted to make a specific reference, I incorporated it into the text. I think now, several years on, things have changed, with very much more literature available to refer to, and more points of view to take into account, so for this new edition I have adopted a more conventional academic style of presentation. As far as content is concerned, the main change has been an expanded chapter 5, which now includes a long section illustrating and discussing the structural features of 'New Englishes'. This too has been the consequence of the much greater availability of descriptive studies of individual varieties than was the case a decade ago. Finally, all population figures and estimates of usage have been updated to the year 2001.

David Crystal
Holyhead

Publisher's note:
The publisher has used its best endeavours to ensure that the URLs for external websites referred to in this book are correct and active at the time of going to press. However, the publisher has no responsibility for the websites and can make no guarantee that a site will remain live or that the content is or will remain appropriate.

Preface to the first edition

————————

It has all happened so quickly. In 1950, any notion of English as a true world language was but a dim, shadowy, theoretical possibility, surrounded by the political uncertainties of the Cold War, and lacking any clear definition or sense of direction. Fifty years on, and World English exists as a political and cultural reality. How could such a dramatic linguistic shift have taken place, in less than a lifetime? And why has English, and not some other language, achieved such a status? These are the questions which this book seeks to answer.

The time is right to address these issues. Thanks to progress in sociolinguistics, we now know a great deal about the social and cultural circumstances which govern language status and change, and several encyclopedic surveys have made available detailed information about world language use. There is also an increasingly urgent need for sensitive discussion. In several countries, the role of English has become politically contentious, and arguments have raged about its current and future status. Have matters developed to the point where the rise of English as a world language is unstoppable? To debate this question, we need to be aware of the factors which will influence the outcome.

It is difficult to write a book on this topic without it being interpreted as a political statement. Because there is no more intimate or more sensitive an index of identity than language, the subject is easily politicized, as it has been in such diverse locations as India,

Malaysia, and the USA. A detached account is all the more desirable, and this is what I have tried to write in these pages, partly based on the historical research I carried out for my *Cambridge encyclopedia of the English language*, but extending this to provide a fuller and more focused analysis of the cultural factors involved. I have thus tried to tell the story of World English objectively, without taking sides on political issues, and without adopting the kind of triumphalist tone which is unfortunately all too common when people write on English in English.

But authors should always tell their readership where they stand, when dealing with contentious topics, hence the following summary. I firmly believe in two linguistic principles, which some people see as contradictory, but which for me are two sides of the one coin.

• I believe in the fundamental value of multilingualism, as an amazing world resource which presents us with different perspectives and insights, and thus enables us to reach a more profound understanding of the nature of the human mind and spirit. In my ideal world, everyone would be at least bi-lingual. I myself live in a community where two languages – Welsh and English – exist side by side, and I have cause to reflect every day on the benefits which come from being part of two cultures. A large part of my academic life, as a researcher in general linguistics, has been devoted to persuading people to take language and languages seriously, so that as much as possible of our linguistic heritage can be preserved.

• I believe in the fundamental value of a common language, as an amazing world resource which presents us with unprecedented possibilities for mutual understanding, and thus enables us to find fresh opportunities for international cooperation. In my ideal world, everyone would have fluent command of a single world language. I am already in the fortunate position of being a fluent user of the language which is most in contention for this role, and have cause to reflect every day on the benefits of having it at my disposal. A large part of my academic life, as a specialist in applied English linguistics, has been devoted to making these benefits available to others, so that the legacy of an unfavoured linguistic heritage should not lead inevitably to disadvantage.

We need to take both principles on board if we are to make any progress towards the kind of peaceful and tolerant society which most people dream about. The first principle fosters historical identity and promotes a climate of mutual respect. The second principle fosters cultural opportunity and promotes a climate of international intelligibility. I hate it when people turn these principles against each other, seeing them as contradictory rather than complementary; but I can perfectly well understand why it happens. I am no innocent in the real bilingual world. Living in a bilingual community as I do, and (when I'm not being a linguist) being the director of a bicultural arts centre, I am very well aware of the problems posed by limited financial resources, conflicts of interest, and downright intolerance. I have had my share of heated arguments with government authorities, local politicians, and national grant-awarding bodies over the question of how to arrive at a sensible and sensitive balance between the two principles, in their local application to the situation in Wales. So I am under no illusions about how difficult it is to achieve a consensus on such deep-rooted matters. But a search for balance and consensus there must always be, in a civilized society, and this need becomes even more critical at a world level, where the resources for mutual harm, as a consequence of failure, are so much greater.

I have written *English as a global language* as a contribution towards this long-term goal, but I cannot take the credit for first seeing the need for such a book. The suggestion in fact came from Mauro E. Mujica, chairman of US English, the largest organization which has been campaigning for English to be made the official language of the USA. He wanted to have a book which would explain to the members of his organization, in a succinct and factual way, and without political bias, why English has achieved such a worldwide status. I could not find such a book, nor did my own previous accounts of the history of the language give a comprehensive account of the social-historical factors involved. I therefore decided to research a short account for private circulation among his membership, and the present book is a heavily reworked, retitled, and much expanded version of that – now including, for example, a separate section on the 'official English' debate in the USA and further material on the use of English on the Internet. Many other revisions derive from suggestions made by a group of British and American academic reviewers of the typescript, commissioned by my publisher, Cambridge University Press, about ways in which the range and balance of the book might be improved; and *English as a global language* has benefited greatly from their input. I am also grateful to Randolph Quirk, especially for his suggestions about ways of improving the statistical picture presented in chapter 2, and to Geoffrey Nunberg for comments which have helped my understanding of the US situation, and for sending me some unpublished observations relating to the Internet, for use in chapter 4.

For some, of course, the mere mention of any political organization, in the natural history of a project, is enough to bias its content. I should therefore make it very clear that this book has not been written according to any political agenda. I would have written exactly the same work if the initial idea had come from an organization on the other side of the US political linguistic divide. *English as a global language* simply asks three questions: what makes a world language? why is English the leading candidate? and will it continue to hold this position? An account of the relevant facts and factors can be of benefit to anyone with an interest in language matters, whatever their political views, and it is this which I hope the book has been able to achieve.

David Crystal
Holyhead

1
Why a global language?

'English is the global language.'

A headline of this kind must have appeared in a thousand newspapers and magazines in recent years. 'English Rules' is an actual example, presenting to the world an uncomplicated scenario suggesting the universality of the language's spread and the likelihood of its continuation.[1] A statement prominently displayed in the body of the associated article, memorable chiefly for its alliterative ingenuity, reinforces the initial impression: 'The British Empire may be in full retreat with the handover of Hong Kong. But from Bengal to Belize and Las Vegas to Lahore, the language of the sceptred isle is rapidly becoming the first global lingua franca.' Millennial retrospectives and prognostications continued in the same vein, with several major newspapers and magazines finding in the subject of the English language an apt symbol for the themes of globalization, diversification, progress and identity addressed in their special editions.[2] Television programmes and series, too, addressed the issue, and achieved world-wide audiences.[3] Certainly, by the turn of the century, the topic must have made contact

---

[1] *Globe and Mail*, Toronto, 12 July 1997.   [2] Ryan (1999).
[3] For example, *Back to Babel*, a four-part (four-hour) series made in 2001 by Infonation, the film-making centre within the British Foreign and Commonwealth Office, had sold to sixty-four countries by 2002. The series was notable for its range of interviews eliciting the attitudes towards English of users in several countries. It was also the first series to devote a significant

1

with millions of popular intuitions at a level which had simply not existed a decade before.

These are the kinds of statement which seem so obvious that most people would give them hardly a second thought. Of course English is a global language, they would say. You hear it on television spoken by politicians from all over the world. Wherever you travel, you see English signs and advertisements. Whenever you enter a hotel or restaurant in a foreign city, they will understand English, and there will be an English menu. Indeed, if there is anything to wonder about at all, they might add, it is why such headlines should still be newsworthy.

But English **is** news. The language continues to make news daily in many countries. And the headline **isn't** stating the obvious. For what does it mean, exactly? Is it saying that everyone in the world speaks English? This is certainly not true, as we shall see. Is it saying, then, that every country in the world recognizes English as an official language? This is not true either. So what does it mean to say that a language is a global language? Why is English the language which is usually cited in this connection? How did the situation arise? And could it change? Or is it the case that, once a language becomes a global language, it is there for ever?

These are fascinating questions to explore, whether your first language is English or not. If English is your mother tongue, you may have mixed feelings about the way English is spreading around the world. You may feel pride, that your language is the one which has been so successful; but your pride may be tinged with concern, when you realize that people in other countries may not want to use the language in the same way that you do, and are changing it to suit themselves. We are all sensitive to the way other people use (it is often said, abuse) 'our' language. Deeply held feelings of ownership begin to be questioned. Indeed, if there is one predictable consequence of a language becoming a global language, it is that nobody owns it any more. Or rather, everyone who has learned it now owns it – 'has a share in it' might be more

---

part of a programme to the consequences for endangered languages (see below, p. 20). The series became available, with extra footage, on DVD in 2002: www.infonation.org.uk.

accurate – and has the right to use it in the way they want. This fact alone makes many people feel uncomfortable, even vaguely resentful. 'Look what the Americans have done to English' is a not uncommon comment found in the letter-columns of the British press. But similar comments can be heard in the USA when people encounter the sometimes striking variations in English which are emerging all over the world.

And if English is not your mother tongue, you may still have mixed feelings about it. You may be strongly motivated to learn it, because you know it will put you in touch with more people than any other language; but at the same time you know it will take a great deal of effort to master it, and you may begrudge that effort. Having made progress, you will feel pride in your achievement, and savour the communicative power you have at your disposal, but may none the less feel that mother-tongue speakers of English have an unfair advantage over you. And if you live in a country where the survival of your own language is threatened by the success of English, you may feel envious, resentful, or angry. You may strongly object to the naivety of the populist account, with its simplistic and often suggestively triumphalist tone.

These feelings are natural, and would arise whichever language emerged as a global language. They are feelings which give rise to fears, whether real or imaginary, and fears lead to conflict. Language marches, language hunger-strikes, language rioting and language deaths are a fact, in several countries. Political differences over language economics, education, laws and rights are a daily encounter for millions. Language is always in the news, and the nearer a language moves to becoming a global language, the more newsworthy it is. So how does a language come to achieve global status?

What is a global language?

A language achieves a genuinely global status when it develops a special role that is recognized in every country. This might seem like stating the obvious, but it is not, for the notion of 'special role' has many facets. Such a role will be most evident in countries where large numbers of the people speak the language as a mother tongue – in the case of English, this would mean the USA, Canada, Britain, Ireland, Australia, New Zealand, South Africa, several Caribbean countries and a sprinkling of other territories. However, no language has ever been spoken by a mother-tongue majority in more than a few countries (Spanish leads, in this respect, in some twenty countries, chiefly in Latin America), so mother-tongue use by itself cannot give a language global status. To achieve such a status, a language has to be taken up by other countries around the world. They must decide to give it a special place within their communities, even though they may have few (or no) mother-tongue speakers.

There are two main ways in which this can be done. Firstly, a language can be made the official language of a country, to be used as a medium of communication in such domains as government, the law courts, the media, and the educational system. To get on in these societies, it is essential to master the official language as early in life as possible. Such a language is often described as a 'second language', because it is seen as a complement to a person's mother tongue, or 'first language'.[4] The role of an official language is today best illustrated by English, which now has some kind of special status in over seventy countries, such as Ghana, Nigeria, India, Singapore and Vanuatu. (A complete list is given at the end of chapter 2.) This is far more than the status achieved by any other language – though French, German, Spanish, Russian, and Arabic are among those which have also developed a considerable official use. New political decisions on the matter continue to be made: for example, Rwanda gave English official status in 1996.

Secondly, a language can be made a priority in a country's foreign-language teaching, even though this language has no official status. It becomes the language which children are most likely to be taught when they arrive in school, and the one most available

---

[4] The term 'second language' needs to be used with caution – as indeed do all terms relating to language status. The most important point to note is that in many parts of the world the term is not related to official status, but simply reflects a notion of competence or usefulness. There is a long-established tradition for the term within the British sphere of influence, but there is no comparable history in the USA.

to adults who – for whatever reason – never learned it, or learned it badly, in their early educational years. Russian, for example, held privileged status for many years among the countries of the former Soviet Union. Mandarin Chinese continues to play an important role in South-east Asia. English is now the language most widely taught as a foreign language – in over 100 countries, such as China, Russia, Germany, Spain, Egypt and Brazil – and in most of these countries it is emerging as the chief foreign language to be encountered in schools, often displacing another language in the process. In 1996, for example, English replaced French as the chief foreign language in schools in Algeria (a former French colony).

In reflecting on these observations, it is important to note that there are several ways in which a language can be official. It may be the sole official language of a country, or it may share this status with other languages. And it may have a 'semi-official' status, being used only in certain domains, or taking second place to other languages while still performing certain official roles. Many countries formally acknowledge a language's status in their constitution (e.g. India); some make no special mention of it (e.g. Britain). In certain countries, the question of whether the special status should be legally recognized is a source of considerable controversy – notably, in the USA (see chapter 5).

Similarly, there is great variation in the reasons for choosing a particular language as a favoured foreign language: they include historical tradition, political expediency, and the desire for commercial, cultural or technological contact. Also, even when chosen, the 'presence' of the language can vary greatly, depending on the extent to which a government or foreign-aid agency is prepared to give adequate financial support to a language-teaching policy. In a well-supported environment, resources will be devoted to helping people have access to the language and learn it, through the media, libraries, schools, and institutes of higher education. There will be an increase in the number and quality of teachers able to teach the language. Books, tapes, computers, telecommunication systems and all kinds of teaching materials will be increasingly available. In many countries, however, lack of government support, or a shortage of foreign aid, has hindered the achievement of language-teaching goals.

Distinctions such as those between 'first', 'second' and 'foreign' language status are useful, but we must be careful not to give them a simplistic interpretation. In particular, it is important to avoid interpreting the distinction between 'second' and 'foreign' language use as a difference in fluency or ability. Although we might expect people from a country where English has some sort of official status to be more competent in the language than those where it has none, simply on grounds of greater exposure, it turns out that this is not always so. We should note, for example, the very high levels of fluency demonstrated by a wide range of speakers from the Scandinavian countries and the Netherlands. But we must also beware introducing too sharp a distinction between first-language speakers and the others, especially in a world where children are being born to parents who communicate with each other through a lingua franca learned as a foreign language. In the Emirates a few years ago, for example, I met a couple – a German oil industrialist and a Malaysian – who had courted through their only common language, English, and decided to bring up their child with English as the primary language of the home. So here is a baby learning English as a foreign language as its mother tongue. There are now many such cases around the world, and they raise a question over the contribution that these babies will one day make to the language, once they grow up to be important people, for their intuitions about English will inevitably be different from those of traditional native speakers.

These points add to the complexity of the present-day world English situation, but they do not alter the fundamental point. Because of the three-pronged development – of first-language, second-language, and foreign-language speakers – it is inevitable that a global language will eventually come to be used by more people than any other language. English has already reached this stage. The statistics collected in chapter 2 suggest that about a quarter of the world's population is already fluent or competent in English, and this figure is steadily growing – in the early 2000s that means around 1.5 billion people. No other language can match this growth. Even Chinese, found in eight different spoken languages, but unified by a common writing system, is known to 'only' some 1.1 billion.

What makes a global language?

Why a language becomes a global language has little to do with the number of people who speak it. It is much more to do with who those speakers are. Latin became an international language throughout the Roman Empire, but this was not because the Romans were more numerous than the peoples they subjugated. They were simply more powerful. And later, when Roman military power declined, Latin remained for a millennium as the international language of education, thanks to a different sort of power – the ecclesiastical power of Roman Catholicism.

There is the closest of links between language dominance and economic, technological, and cultural power, too, and this relationship will become increasingly clear as the history of English is told (see chapters 2 –4). Without a strong power-base, of whatever kind, no language can make progress as an international medium of communication. Language has no independent existence, living in some sort of mystical space apart from the people who speak it. Language exists only in the brains and mouths and ears and hands and eyes of its users. When they succeed, on the international stage, their language succeeds. When they fail, their language fails.

This point may seem obvious, but it needs to be made at the outset, because over the years many popular and misleading beliefs have grown up about why a language should become internationally successful. It is quite common to hear people claim that a language is a paragon, on account of its perceived aesthetic qualities, clarity of expression, literary power, or religious standing. Hebrew, Greek, Latin, Arabic and French are among those which at various times have been lauded in such terms, and English is no exception. It is often suggested, for example, that there must be something inherently beautiful or logical about the structure of English, in order to explain why it is now so widely used. 'It has less grammar than other languages', some have suggested. 'English doesn't have a lot of endings on its words, nor do we have to remember the difference between masculine, feminine, and neuter gender, so it must be easier to learn'. In 1848, a reviewer in the British periodical *The Athenaeum* wrote:

In its easiness of grammatical construction, in its paucity of inflection, in its almost total disregard of the distinctions of gender excepting those of nature, in the simplicity and precision of its terminations and auxiliary verbs, not less than in the majesty, vigour and copiousness of its expression, our mother-tongue seems well adapted by *organization* to become the language of the world.

Such arguments are misconceived. Latin was once a major international language, despite its many inflectional endings and gender differences. French, too, has been such a language, despite its nouns being masculine or feminine; and so – at different times and places – have the heavily inflected Greek, Arabic, Spanish and Russian. Ease of learning has nothing to do with it. Children of all cultures learn to talk over more or less the same period of time, regardless of the differences in the grammar of their languages. And as for the notion that English has 'no grammar' – a claim that is risible to anyone who has ever had to learn it as a foreign language – the point can be dismissed by a glance at any of the large twentieth-century reference grammars. The *Comprehensive grammar of the English language*, for example, contains 1,800 pages and some 3,500 points requiring grammatical exposition.[5]

This is not to deny that a language may have certain properties which make it internationally appealing. For example, learners sometimes comment on the 'familiarity' of English vocabulary, deriving from the way English has over the centuries borrowed thousands of new words from the languages with which it has been in contact. The 'welcome' given to foreign vocabulary places English in contrast to some languages (notably, French) which have tried to keep it out, and gives it a cosmopolitan character which many see as an advantage for a global language. From a lexical point of view, English is in fact far more a Romance than a Germanic language. And there have been comments made about other structural aspects, too, such as the absence in English

---

[5] Largely points to do with syntax, of course, rather than the morphological emphasis which is what many people, brought up in the Latinate tradition, think grammar to be about. The figure of 3,500 is derived from the index which I compiled for Quirk, Greenbaum, Leech and Svartvik (1985), excluding entries which related solely to lexical items.

grammar of a system of coding social class differences, which can make the language appear more 'democratic' to those who speak a language (e.g. Javanese) that does express an intricate system of class relationships. But these supposed traits of appeal are incidental, and need to be weighed against linguistic features which would seem to be internationally much less desirable – notably, in the case of English, the accumulated irregularities of its spelling system.

A language does not become a global language because of its intrinsic structural properties, or because of the size of its vocabulary, or because it has been a vehicle of a great literature in the past, or because it was once associated with a great culture or religion. These are all factors which can motivate someone to learn a language, of course, but none of them alone, or in combination, can ensure a language's world spread. Indeed, such factors cannot even guarantee survival as a living language – as is clear from the case of Latin, learned today as a classical language by only a scholarly and religious few. Correspondingly, inconvenient structural properties (such as awkward spelling) do not stop a language achieving international status either.

A language has traditionally become an international language for one chief reason: the power of its people – especially their political and military power. The explanation is the same throughout history. Why did Greek become a language of international communication in the Middle East over 2,000 years ago? Not because of the intellects of Plato and Aristotle: the answer lies in the swords and spears wielded by the armies of Alexander the Great. Why did Latin become known throughout Europe? Ask the legions of the Roman Empire. Why did Arabic come to be spoken so widely across northern Africa and the Middle East? Follow the spread of Islam, carried along by the force of the Moorish armies from the eighth century. Why did Spanish, Portuguese, and French find their way into the Americas, Africa and the Far East? Study the colonial policies of the Renaissance kings and queens, and the way these policies were ruthlessly implemented by armies and navies all over the known world. The history of a global language can be traced through the successful expeditions of its soldier/sailor speakers. And English, as we shall see in chapter 2, has been no exception.

But international language dominance is not solely the result of military might. It may take a militarily powerful nation to establish a language, but it takes an economically powerful one to maintain and expand it. This has always been the case, but it became a particularly critical factor in the nineteenth and twentieth centuries, with economic developments beginning to operate on a global scale, supported by the new communication technologies – telegraph, telephone, radio – and fostering the emergence of massive multinational organizations. The growth of competitive industry and business brought an explosion of international marketing and advertising. The power of the press reached unprecedented levels, soon to be surpassed by the broadcasting media, with their ability to cross national boundaries with electromagnetic ease. Technology, chiefly in the form of movies and records, fuelled new mass entertainment industries which had a worldwide impact. The drive to make progress in science and technology fostered an international intellectual and research environment which gave scholarship and further education a high profile.

Any language at the centre of such an explosion of international activity would suddenly have found itself with a global status. And English, as we shall see in chapters 3 and 4, was apparently 'in the right place at the right time' (p. 78). By the beginning of the nineteenth century, Britain had become the world's leading industrial and trading country. By the end of the century, the population of the USA (then approaching 100 million) was larger than that of any of the countries of western Europe, and its economy was the most productive and the fastest growing in the world. British political imperialism had sent English around the globe, during the nineteenth century, so that it was a language 'on which the sun never sets'.[6] During the twentieth century, this world presence was maintained and promoted almost single-handedly through the economic supremacy of the new American superpower. Economics replaced politics as the chief driving force. And the language behind the US dollar was English.

[6] An expression adapted from the nineteenth-century aphorism about the extent of the British Empire. It continued to be used in the twentieth century, for example by Randolph Quirk (1985: 1).

Why do we need a global language?

Translation has played a central (though often unrecognized) role in human interaction for thousands of years. When monarchs or ambassadors met on the international stage, there would invariably be interpreters present. But there are limits to what can be done in this way. The more a community is linguistically mixed, the less it can rely on individuals to ensure communication between different groups. In communities where only two or three languages are in contact, bilingualism (or trilingualism) is a possible solution, for most young children can acquire more than one language with unselfconscious ease. But in communities where there are many languages in contact, as in much of Africa and South-east Asia, such a natural solution does not readily apply.

The problem has traditionally been solved by finding a language to act as a *lingua franca*, or 'common language'. Sometimes, when communities begin to trade with each other, they communicate by adopting a simplified language, known as a *pidgin*, which combines elements of their different languages.[7] Many such pidgin languages survive today in territories which formerly belonged to the European colonial nations, and act as lingua francas; for example, West African Pidgin English is used extensively between several ethnic groups along the West African coast. Sometimes an indigenous language emerges as a lingua franca – usually the language of the most powerful ethnic group in the area, as in the case of Mandarin Chinese. The other groups then learn this language with varying success, and thus become to some degree bilingual. But most often, a language is accepted from outside the community, such as English or French, because of the political, economic, or religious influence of a foreign power.

The geographical extent to which a lingua franca can be used is entirely governed by political factors. Many lingua francas extend over quite small domains – between a few ethnic groups in one part of a single country, or linking the trading populations of just a few countries, as in the West African case. By contrast, Latin was a lingua franca throughout the whole of the Roman Empire – at

[7] For the rise of pidgin Englishes, see Todd (1984).

11

least, at the level of government (very few 'ordinary' people in the subjugated domains would have spoken much Latin). And in modern times Swahili, Arabic, Spanish, French, English, Hindi, Portuguese and several other languages have developed a major international role as a lingua franca, in limited areas of the world.

The prospect that a lingua franca might be needed for the **whole** world is something which has emerged strongly only in the twentieth century, and since the 1950s in particular. The chief international forum for political communication – the United Nations – dates only from 1945. Since then, many international bodies have come into being, such as the World Bank (also 1945), UNESCO and UNICEF (both 1946), the World Health Organization (1948) and the International Atomic Energy Agency (1957). Never before have so many countries (around 190, in the case of some UN bodies) been represented in single meeting-places. At a more restricted level, multinational regional or political groupings have come into being, such as the Commonwealth and the European Union. The pressure to adopt a single lingua franca, to facilitate communication in such contexts, is considerable, the alternative being expensive and impracticable multi-way translation facilities.

Usually a small number of languages have been designated official languages for an organization's activities: for example, the UN was established with five official languages – English, French, Spanish, Russian and Chinese. There is now a widespread view that it makes sense to try to reduce the numbers of languages involved in world bodies, if only to cut down on the vast amount of interpretation/translation and clerical work required. Half the budget of an international organization can easily get swallowed up in translation costs. But trimming a translation budget is never easy, as obviously no country likes the thought of its language being given a reduced international standing. Language choice is always one of the most sensitive issues facing a planning committee. The common situation is one where a committee does not have to be involved – where all the participants at an international meeting automatically use a single language, as a utilitarian measure (a 'working language'), because it is one which they have all come to learn for separate reasons. This situation seems to be

12

slowly becoming a reality in meetings around the world, as general competence in English grows.

The need for a global language is particularly appreciated by the international academic and business communities, and it is here that the adoption of a single lingua franca is most in evidence, both in lecture-rooms and board-rooms, as well as in thousands of individual contacts being made daily all over the globe. A conversation over the Internet (see chapter 4) between academic physicists in Sweden, Italy, and India is at present practicable only if a common language is available. A situation where a Japanese company director arranges to meet German and Saudi Arabian contacts in a Singapore hotel to plan a multi-national deal would not be impossible, if each plugged in to a 3-way translation support system, but it would be far more complicated than the alternative, which is for each to make use of the same language.

As these examples suggest, the growth in international contacts has been largely the result of two separate developments. The physicists would not be talking so conveniently to each other at all without the technology of modern communication. And the business contacts would be unable to meet so easily in Singapore without the technology of air transportation. The availability of both these facilities in the twentieth century, more than anything else, provided the circumstances needed for a global language to grow.

People have, in short, become more mobile, both physically and electronically. Annual airline statistics show that steadily increasing numbers are finding the motivation as well as the means to transport themselves physically around the globe, and sales of faxes, modems, and personal computers show an even greater increase in those prepared to send their ideas in words and images electronically. It is now possible, using electronic mail, to copy a message to hundreds of locations all over the world virtually simultaneously. It is just as easy for me to send a message from my house in the small town of Holyhead, North Wales, to a friend in Washington as it is to get the same message to someone living just a few streets away from me. In fact, it is probably easier. That is why people so often talk, these days, of the 'global village'.

These trends would be taking place, presumably, if only a handful of countries were talking to each other. What has been so impressive about the developments which have taken place since the 1950s is that they have affected, to a greater or lesser extent, every country in the world, and that so many countries have come to be involved. There is no nation now which does not have some level of accessibility using telephone, radio, television, and air transport, though facilities such as fax, electronic mail and the Internet are much less widely available.

The scale and recency of the development has to be appreciated. In 1945, the United Nations began life with 51 member states. By 1956 this had risen to 80 members. But the independence movements which began at that time led to a massive increase in the number of new nations during the next decade, and this process continued steadily into the 1990s, following the collapse of the USSR. There were 190 member states in 2002 – nearly four times as many as there were fifty years ago. And the trend may not yet be over, given the growth of so many regional nationalistic movements worldwide.

There are no precedents in human history for what happens to languages, in such circumstances of rapid change. There has never been a time when so many nations were needing to talk to each other so much. There has never been a time when so many people wished to travel to so many places. There has never been such a strain placed on the conventional resources of translating and interpreting. Never has the need for more widespread bilingualism been greater, to ease the burden placed on the professional few. And never has there been a more urgent need for a global language.

What are the dangers of a global language?

The benefits which would flow from the existence of a global language are considerable; but several commentators have pointed to possible risks.[8] Perhaps a global language will cultivate an elite monolingual linguistic class, more complacent and dismissive in

---

[8] These risks, and all the associated points discussed in this section, are given a full treatment in the companion volume to this one, *Language death* (Crystal 2000).

their attitudes towards other languages. Perhaps those who have such a language at their disposal – and especially those who have it as a mother-tongue – will be more able to think and work quickly in it, and to manipulate it to their own advantage at the expense of those who do not have it, thus maintaining in a linguistic guise the chasm between rich and poor. Perhaps the presence of a global language will make people lazy about learning other languages, or reduce their opportunities to do so. Perhaps a global language will hasten the disappearance of minority languages, or – the ultimate threat – make **all** other languages unnecessary. 'A person needs only one language to talk to someone else', it is sometimes argued, 'and once a world language is in place, other languages will simply die away'. Linked with all this is the unpalatable face of linguistic triumphalism – the danger that some people will celebrate one language's success at the expense of others.

It is important to face up to these fears, and to recognize that they are widely held. There is no shortage of mother-tongue English speakers who believe in an evolutionary view of language ('let the fittest survive, and if the fittest happens to be English, then so be it') or who refer to the present global status of the language as a 'happy accident'. There are many who think that all language learning is a waste of time. And many more who see nothing wrong with the vision that a world with just one language in it would be a very good thing. For some, such a world would be one of unity and peace, with all misunderstanding washed away – a widely expressed hope underlying the movements in support of a universal artificial language (such as Esperanto). For others, such a world would be a desirable return to the 'innocence' that must have been present among human beings in the days before the Tower of Babel.[9]

It is difficult to deal with anxieties which are so speculative, or, in the absence of evidence, to determine whether anything can

---

[9] The Babel myth is particularly widely held, because of its status as part of a biblical narrative (Genesis, chapter 11). Even in biblical terms, however, there is no ground for saying that Babel introduced multilingualism as a 'curse' or 'punishment'. Languages were already in existence before Babel, as we learn from Genesis, chapter 10, where the sons of Japheth are listed 'according to their countries and each of their languages'. See Eco (1995).

be done to reduce or eliminate them. The last point can be quite briefly dismissed: the use of a single language by a community is no guarantee of social harmony or mutual understanding, as has been repeatedly seen in world history (e.g. the American Civil War, the Spanish Civil War, the Vietnam War, former Yugoslavia, contemporary Northern Ireland); nor does the presence of more than one language within a community necessitate civil strife, as seen in several successful examples of peaceful multilingual coexistence (e.g. Finland, Singapore, Switzerland). The other points, however, need to be taken more slowly, to appreciate the alternative perspective. The arguments are each illustrated with reference to English – but the same arguments would apply whatever language was in the running for global status.

• *Linguistic power*   Will those who speak a global language as a mother tongue automatically be in a position of power compared with those who have to learn it as an official or foreign language? The risk is certainly real. It is possible, for example, that scientists who do not have English as a mother tongue will take longer to assimilate reports in English compared with their mother-tongue colleagues, and will as a consequence have less time to carry out their own creative work. It is possible that people who write up their research in languages other than English will have their work ignored by the international community. It is possible that senior managers who do not have English as a mother tongue, and who find themselves working for English-language companies in such parts of the world as Europe or Africa, could find themselves at a disadvantage compared with their mother-tongue colleagues, especially when meetings involve the use of informal speech. There is already anecdotal evidence to suggest that these things happen.

However, if proper attention is paid to the question of language learning, the problem of disadvantage dramatically diminishes. If a global language is taught early enough, from the time that children begin their full-time education, and if it is maintained continuously and resourced well, the kind of linguistic competence which emerges in due course is a real and powerful bilingualism, indistinguishable from that found in any speaker who has encountered the language since birth. These are enormous 'ifs',

16

with costly financial implications, and it is therefore not surprising that this kind of control is currently achieved by only a minority of non-native learners of any language; but the fact that it is achievable (as evidenced repeatedly by English speakers from such countries as Denmark, Sweden and the Netherlands) indicates that there is nothing inevitable about the disadvantage scenario. It is worth reflecting, at this point, on the notion that children are born ready for bilingualism. Some two-thirds of the children on earth grow up in a bilingual environment, and develop competence in it. There is a naturalness with which they assimilate another language, once they are regularly exposed to it, which is the envy of adults. It is an ability which seems to die away as children reach their teens, and much academic debate has been devoted to the question of why this should be (the question of 'critical periods').[10] There is however widespread agreement that, if we want to take the task of foreign language learning seriously, one of the key principles is 'the earlier the better'. And when that task **is** taken seriously, with reference to the acquisition of a global language, the elitism argument evaporates.

• *Linguistic complacency* Will a global language eliminate the motivation for adults to learn other languages? Here too the problem is real enough. Clear signs of linguistic complacency, common observation suggests, are already present in the archetypal British or American tourist who travels the world assuming that everyone speaks English, and that it is somehow the fault of the local people if they do not. The stereotype of an English tourist repeatedly asking a foreign waiter for tea in a loud 'read my lips' voice is too near the reality to be comfortable. There seems already to be a genuine, widespread lack of motivation to learn other languages, fuelled partly by lack of money and opportunity, but also by lack of interest, and this might well be fostered by the increasing presence of English as a global language.

It is important to appreciate that we are dealing here with questions of attitude or state of mind rather than questions of

---

[10] For bilingual acquisition, see De Houwer (1995), Baker and Prys Jones (1998).

ability – though it is the latter which is often cited as the explanation. 'I'm no good at languages' is probably the most widely heard apology for not making any effort at all to acquire even a basic knowledge of a new language. Commonly, this self-denigration derives from an unsatisfactory language learning experience in school: the speaker is perhaps remembering a poor result in school examinations – which may reflect no more than an unsuccessful teaching approach or a not unusual breakdown in teacher–adolescent relationships. 'I never got on with my French teacher' is another typical comment. But this does not stop people going on to generalize that 'the British (or the Americans, etc.) are not very good at learning languages'.

These days, there are clear signs of growing awareness, within English-speaking communities, of the need to break away from the traditional monolingual bias.[11] In economically hard-pressed times, success in boosting exports and attracting foreign investment can depend on subtle factors, and sensitivity to the language spoken by a country's potential foreign partners is known to be particularly influential.[12] At least at the levels of business and industry, many firms have begun to make fresh efforts in this direction. But at grass-roots tourist level, too, there are signs of a growing respect for other cultures, and a greater readiness to engage in language learning. Language attitudes are changing all the time, and more and more people are discovering, to their great delight, that they are not at all bad at picking up a foreign language.

In particular, statements from influential politicians and administrators are beginning to be made which are helping to foster a fresh climate of opinion about the importance of language learning. A good example is an address given in 1996 by the former secretary-general of the Commonwealth, Sir Sridath

[11] The awareness is by no means restricted to English-speaking communities, as was demonstrated by the spread of activities associated with the European Year of Languages, 2001 (European Commission (2002a)).

[12] For economic arguments in support of multilingualism and foreign language learning, see the 1996 issue of the *International Journal of the Sociology of Language* on 'Economic Approaches to Language and Language Planning'; also Coulmas (1992).

Ramphal. His title, 'World language: opportunities, challenges, responsibilities', itself contains a corrective to triumphalist thinking, and his text repeatedly argues against it:[13]

It is all too easy to make your way in the world linguistically with English as your mother tongue...We become lazy about learning other languages...We all have to make a greater effort. English may be the world language; but it is not the world's only language and if we are to be good global neighbours we shall have to be less condescending to the languages of the world – more assiduous in cultivating acquaintance with them.

It remains to be seen whether such affirmations of good will have long-term effect. In the meantime, it is salutary to read some of the comparative statistics about foreign language learning. For example, a European Business Survey by Grant Thornton reported in 1996 that 90 per cent of businesses in Belgium, The Netherlands, Luxembourg and Greece had an executive able to negotiate in another language, whereas only 38 per cent of British companies had someone who could do so. In 2002 the figures remained high for most European countries in the survey, but had fallen to 29 per cent in Britain.[14] The UK-based Centre for Information on Language Teaching and Research found that a third of British exporters miss opportunities because of poor language skills.[15] And English-monolingual companies are increasingly encountering language difficulties as they try to expand in those areas of the world thought to have greatest prospects of growth, such as East Asia, South America, and Eastern Europe – areas where English has traditionally had a relatively low presence. The issues are beginning to be addressed – for example, many Australian schools now teach Japanese as the first foreign language, and both the USA and UK are now paying more attention to Spanish (which, in terms of mother-tongue use, is growing more rapidly than English) – but we are still a long way from a world where the economic and other arguments have universally

---

[13] Ramphal (1996).   [14] Grant Thornton (2002).
[15] For a recent statement, see CILT (2002).

persuaded the English-speaking nations to renounce their linguistic insularity.

• *Linguistic death* Will the emergence of a global language hasten the disappearance of minority languages and cause widespread language death? To answer this question, we must first establish a general perspective. The processes of language domination and loss have been known throughout linguistic history, and exist independently of the emergence of a global language. No one knows how many languages have died since humans became able to speak, but it must be thousands. In many of these cases, the death has been caused by an ethnic group coming to be assimilated within a more dominant society, and adopting its language. The situation continues today, though the matter is being discussed with increasing urgency because of the unprecedented rate at which indigenous languages are being lost, especially in North America, Brazil, Australia, Indonesia and parts of Africa. At least 50 per cent of the world's 6,000 or so living languages will die out within the next century.[16]

This is indeed an intellectual and social tragedy. When a language dies, so much is lost. Especially in languages which have never been written down, or which have been written down only recently, language is the repository of the history of a people. It is their identity. Oral testimony, in the form of sagas, folktales, songs, rituals, proverbs, and many other practices, provides us with a unique view of our world and a unique canon of literature. It is their legacy to the rest of humanity. Once lost, it can never be recaptured. The argument is similar to that used in relation to the conservation of species and the environment. The documentation and – where practicable – conservation of languages is also a priority, and it was good to see in the 1990s a number of international organizations being formed with the declared aim of recording for posterity as many endangered languages as possible.[17]

---

[16] This is an average of the estimates which have been proposed. For a detailed examination of these estimates, see Crystal (2000: chapter 1).

[17] These organizations include The International Clearing House for Endangered Languages in Tokyo, The Foundation for Endangered Languages

However, the emergence of any one language as global has only a limited causal relationship to this unhappy state of affairs. Whether Sorbian survives in Germany or Galician in Spain has to do with the local political and economic history of those countries, and with the regional dominance of German and Spanish respectively, and bears no immediate relationship to the standing of German or Spanish on the world stage.[18] Nor is it easy to see how the arrival of English as a global language could directly influence the future of these or many other minority languages. An effect is likely only in those areas where English has itself come to be the dominant first language, such as in North America, Australia and the Celtic parts of the British Isles. The early history of language contact in these areas was indeed one of conquest and assimilation, and the effects on indigenous languages were disastrous. But in more recent times, the emergence of English as a truly global language has, if anything, had the reverse effect – stimulating a stronger response in support of a local language than might otherwise have been the case. Times have changed. Movements for language rights (alongside civil rights in general) have played an important part in several countries, such as in relation to the Maori in New Zealand, the Aboriginal languages of Australia, the Indian languages of Canada and the USA, and some of the Celtic languages. Although often too late, in certain instances the decline of a language has been slowed, and occasionally (as in the case of Welsh) halted.

The existence of vigorous movements in support of linguistic minorities, commonly associated with nationalism, illustrates an important truth about the nature of language in general. The

in the UK, and The Endangered Language Fund in the USA. Contact details for these and similar organizations are given in Crystal (2000: Appendix).

[18] The point can be made even more strongly in such parts of the world as Latin America, where English has traditionally had negligible influence. The hundreds of Amerindian languages which have disappeared in Central and South America have done so as a result of cultures which spoke Spanish and Portuguese, not English. Chinese, Russian, Arabic and other major languages have all had an impact on minority languages throughout their history, and continue to do so. The responsibility for language preservation and revitalization is a shared one.

need for mutual intelligibility, which is part of the argument in favour of a global language, is only one side of the story. The other side is the need for identity – and people tend to underestimate the role of identity when they express anxieties about language injury and death. Language is a major means (some would say the chief means) of showing where we belong, and of distinguishing one social group from another, and all over the world we can see evidence of linguistic divergence rather than convergence. For decades, many people in the countries of former Yugoslavia made use of a common language, Serbo-Croatian. But since the civil wars of the early 1990s, the Serbs have referred to their language as Serbian, the Bosnians to theirs as Bosnian, and the Croats to theirs as Croatian, with each community drawing attention to the linguistic features which are distinctive. A similar situation exists in Scandinavia, where Swedish, Norwegian, and Danish are largely mutually intelligible, but are none the less considered to be different languages.

Arguments about the need for national or cultural identity are often seen as being opposed to those about the need for mutual intelligibility. But this is misleading. It is perfectly possible to develop a situation in which intelligibility and identity happily co-exist. This situation is the familiar one of bilingualism – but a bilingualism where one of the languages within a speaker is the global language, providing access to the world community, and the other is a well-resourced regional language, providing access to a local community. The two functions can be seen as complementary, responding to different needs. And it is because the functions are so different that a world of linguistic diversity can in principle continue to exist in a world united by a common language.

None of this is to deny that the emergence of a global language can influence the structure of other languages – especially by providing a fresh source of loan-words for use by these other languages. Such influences can be welcomed (in which case, people talk about their language being 'varied' and 'enriched') or opposed (in which case, the metaphors are those of 'injury' and 'death'). For example, in recent years, one of the healthiest languages, French, has tried to protect itself by law against what is widely perceived to be the malign influence of English: in official contexts, it is now illegal to use an English word where a French word already exists, even though the usage may have widespread popular support (e.g. *computer* for *ordinateur*). Purist commentators from several other countries have also expressed concern at the way in which English vocabulary – especially that of American English – has come to permeate their high streets and TV programmes. The arguments are carried on with great emotional force. Even though only a tiny part of the lexicon is ever affected in this way, that is enough to arouse the wrath of the prophets of doom. (They usually forget the fact that English itself, over the centuries, has borrowed thousands of words from other languages, and constructed thousands more from the elements of other languages – including *computer*, incidentally, which derives from Latin, the mother-language of French.)[19]

The relationship between the global spread of English and its impact on other languages attracted increasing debate during the 1990s. The fact that it is possible to show a correlation between the rate of English adoption and the demise of minority languages has led some observers to reassert the conclusion that there is a simple causal link between the two phenomena, ignoring the fact that there has been a similar loss of linguistic diversity in parts of the world where English has not had a history of significant presence, such as Latin America, Russia and China. A more deep-rooted process of globalization seems to be at work today, transcending individual language situations. Anachronistic views of linguistic imperialism, which see as important only the power asymmetry between the former colonial nations and the nations of the 'third world', are hopelessly inadequate as an

[19] English has borrowed words from over 350 other languages, and over three-quarters of the English lexicon is actually Classical or Romance in origin. Plainly, the view that to borrow words leads to a language's decline is absurd, given that English has borrowed more words than most. Languages change their character, as a result of such borrowing, of course, and this too upsets purists, who seem unable to appreciate the expressive gains which come from having the option of choosing between lexical alternatives, as in such 'triplets' as (Anglo-Saxon) *kingly*, (French) *royal* and (Latin) *regal*. For further examples, see the classic source, Serjeantson (1935), also Crystal (1995a). See also Görlach (2002).

explanation of linguistic realities.[20] They especially ignore the fact that 'first world' countries with strong languages seem to be under just as much pressure to adopt English, and that some of the harshest attacks on English have come from countries which have no such colonial legacy. When dominant languages feel they are being dominated, something much bigger than a simplistic conception of power relations must be involved.[21]

These other factors, which include the recognition of global interdependence, the desire to have a voice in world affairs, and the value of multilingualism in attracting trade markets, all support the adoption of a functionalist account of English, where the language is seen as a valuable instrument enabling people to achieve particular goals. Local languages continue to perform an important set of functions (chiefly, the expression of local identity) and English is seen as the primary means of achieving a global presence. The approach recognizes the legacy of colonialism, as a matter of historical fact, but the emphasis is now on discontinuities, away from power and towards functional specialization.[22] It is a model which sees English playing a central role in empowering the subjugated and marginalized, and eroding the division between the 'haves' and the 'have nots'. Those who argue for this position have been dismissed as displaying 'naive liberal idealism' and adopting a 'liberal laissez-faire attitude'.[23] Rather, it is the linguistic imperialism position which is naive, disregarding the

---

[20] Two prominent positions are Phillipson (1992) and Pennycook (1994).

[21] The point is also made by Lysandrou and Lysandrou (in press: 3): 'The pace of English language adoption over the past decade or so has been so explosive as to make it difficult if not impossible to accept that those accounts of the phenomenon which focus on power asymmetries can bear the burden of explanation.' It is reinforced by the literature on language endangerment, which has made it very clear that the survival of a language depends largely on factors other than political power (e.g. Brenzinger (1998), Crystal (2000)). Focusing on Africa, for example, Mufwene (2001, 2002) has drawn attention to the many African languages which have lost their vitality because speakers have adopted peer languages that have guaranteed a surer economic survival.

[22] For example, Fishman, Conrad and Rubal-Lopez (1996).

[23] The name-calling is Pennycook's (2001: 56), who uses these phrases with reference to the first edition of the present ('overmarketed' (sic)) book. For a further example of what might euphemistically be called 'debate', see Phillipson (1998/1999) and Crystal (1999/2000).

complex realities of a world in which a historical conception of power relations has to be seen alongside an emerging set of empowering relationships in which English has a new functional role, no longer associated with the political authority it once held.

If working towards the above goal is idealism, then I am happy to be an idealist; however, it is by no means laissez-faire, given the amount of time, energy and money which have been devoted in recent years to language revitalization and related matters. Admittedly, the progress which has been made is tiny compared with the disastrous effects of globalization on global diversity. But to place all the blame on English, and to ignore the more fundamental economic issues that are involved, is, as two recent commentators have put it, 'to attack the wrong target, to indulge in linguistic luddism'.[24] Solutions are more likely to come from the domain of economic policy, not language policy. As Lysandrou and Lysandrou conclude:

If English can facilitate the process of universal dispossession and loss, so can it be turned round and made to facilitate the contrary process of universal empowerment and gain.

Could anything stop a global language?

Any discussion of an emerging global language has to be seen in the political context of global governance as a whole. In January 1995, the Commission on Global Governance published its report, *Our global neighbourhood*.[25] A year later, the Commission's co-chairman, Sridath Ramphal, commented (in the paper referred to on p. 19):

There were, for the most part, people who were pleased that the Report had engaged the central issue of a global community, but they took us to task for not going on – in as they thought in a logical way – to call for a world language. They could not see how the global neighbourhood, the global community, which they acknowledged had come into being, could function effectively without a world language. A neighbourhood

[24] Lysandrou and Lysandrou (in press: 24).
[25] Commission on Global Governance (1995).

25

that can only talk in the tongues of many was not a neighbourhood that was likely to be cohesive or, perhaps, even cooperative . . . And they were right in one respect; but they were wrong in the sense that we **have** a world language. It is not the language of imperialism; it is the language we have seen that has evolved out of a history of which we need not always be proud, but whose legacies we must use to good effect.

And at another place, he comments: 'there is no retreat from English as the world language; no retreat from an English-speaking world'.

Strong political statements of this kind immediately prompt the question, 'Could anything stop a language, once it achieves a global status?' The short answer must be 'yes'. If language dominance is a matter of political and especially economic influence, then a revolution in the balance of global power could have consequences for the choice of global language.[26] There is no shortage of books – chiefly within the genre of science fiction – which foresee a future in which, following some cataclysmic scenario, the universal language is Chinese, Arabic or even some Alien tongue. But to end up with such a scenario, the revolution would indeed have to be cataclysmic, and it is difficult to speculate sensibly about what this might be.[27] Smaller-scale revolutions in the world order would be unlikely to have much effect, given that – as we shall see in later chapters – English is now so widely established that it can no longer be thought of as 'owned' by any single nation.

A rather more plausible scenario is that an alternative method of communication could emerge which would eliminate the need for a global language. The chief candidate here is automatic translation ('machine translation'). If progress in this domain continues to be as rapid as it has been in the past decade, there is a distinct possibility that, within a generation or two, it will be routine for people to communicate with each other directly, using their first languages, with a computer 'taking the strain' between them.

---

[26] Graddol (1998) explores this scenario.
[27] Speculation about the political state of the world leads Dalby (2002) to envision 200 languages remaining in 200 years' time. Janson (2002) takes linguistic speculation to an even more apocalyptic point, reflecting on the state of human language 2 million years from now.

This state of affairs can already be seen, to a limited extent, on the Internet, where some firms are now offering a basic translation service between certain language pairs. A sender types in a message in language X, and a version of it appears on the receiver's screen in language Y. The need for post-editing is still considerable, however, as translation software is currently very limited in its ability to handle idiomatic, stylistic, and several other linguistic features; the machines are nowhere near replacing their human counterparts. Similarly, notwithstanding the remarkable progress in speech recognition and synthesis which has taken place in recent years, the state of the art in real-time speech-to-speech automatic translation is still primitive. The 'Babel fish', inserted into the ear, thus making all spoken languages (in the galaxy) intelligible, is no more than an intriguing concept.[28]

The accuracy and speed of real-time automatic translation is undoubtedly going to improve dramatically in the next twenty-five to fifty years, but it is going to take much longer before this medium becomes so globally widespread, and so economically accessible to all, that is poses a threat to the current availability and appeal of a global language. And during this time frame, all the evidence suggests that the position of English as a global language is going to become stronger. By the time automatic translation matures as a popular communicative medium, that position will very likely have become impregnable. It will be very interesting to see what happens then – whether the presence of a global language will eliminate the demand for world translation services, or whether the economics of automatic translation will so undercut the cost of global language learning that the latter will become otiose. It will be an interesting battle 100 years from now.

A critical era

It is impossible to make confident predictions about the emergence of a global language. There are no precedents for this kind of linguistic growth, other than on a much smaller scale. And the speed with which a global language scenario has arisen is truly

---

[28] Explored by Douglas Adams (1979: chapter 6).

remarkable. Within little more than a generation, we have moved from a situation where a world language was a theoretical possibility to one where it is an evident reality. No government has yet found it possible to plan confidently, in such circumstances. Languages of identity need to be maintained. Access to the emerging global language – widely perceived as a language of opportunity and empowerment – needs to be guaranteed. Both principles demand massive resources. The irony is that the issue is approaching a climax at a time when the world financial climate can least afford it.

Fundamental decisions about priorities have to be made. Those making the decisions need to bear in mind that we may well be approaching a critical moment in human linguistic history. It is possible that a global language will emerge only once. Certainly, as we have seen, after such a language comes to be established it would take a revolution of world-shattering proportions to replace it. And in due course, the last quarter of the twentieth century will be seen as a critical time in the emergence of this global language.

For the reasons presented in the next three chapters, all the signs suggest that this global language will be English. But there is still some way to go before a global lingua franca becomes a universal reality. Despite the remarkable growth in the use of English, at least two-thirds of the world population do not yet use it. In certain parts of the world (most of the states of the former Soviet Union, for example), English has still a very limited presence. And in some countries, increased resources are being devoted to maintaining the role of other languages (such as the use of French in several countries of Africa). Notwithstanding the general world trend, there are many linguistic confrontations still to be resolved.

Governments who wish to play their part in influencing the world's linguistic future should therefore ponder carefully, as they make political decisions and allocate resources for language planning. Now, more than at any time in linguistic history, they need to adopt long-term views, and to plan ahead – whether their interests are to promote English or to develop the use of other languages in their community (or, of course, both). If they miss this linguistic boat, there may be no other.

28

2
Why English? The historical context

—⁓⁓⁓⁓⁓@⁓⁓⁓⁓—

'Why is English the global language, and not some other?' There are two answers to the question: one is geographical-historical; the other is socio-cultural. The geo-historical answer shows how English reached a position of pre-eminence, and this is presented below. The socio-cultural answer explains why it remains so, and this is presented in chapters 3 and 4. The combination of these two strands has brought into existence a language which consists of many varieties, each distinctive in its use of sounds, grammar, and vocabulary, and the implications of this are presented in chapter 5.

The historical account traces the movement of English around the world, beginning with the pioneering voyages to the Americas, Asia, and the Antipodes. It was an expansion which continued with the nineteenth-century colonial developments in Africa and the South Pacific, and which took a significant further step when it was adopted in the mid twentieth century as an official or semi-official language by many newly independent states. English is now represented in every continent, and in islands of the three major oceans – Atlantic (St Helena), Indian (Seychelles) and Pacific (in many islands, such as Fiji and Hawaii). It is this spread of representation which makes the application of the label 'global language' a reality.

The socio-cultural explanation looks at the way people all over the world, in many walks of life, have come to depend on English for their economic and social well-being. The language has penetrated deeply into the international domains of political life, business, safety, communication, entertainment, the media and education. The convenience of having a lingua franca available to serve global human relations and needs has come to be appreciated by millions. Several domains, as we shall see, have come to be totally dependent on it – the computer software industry being a prime example. A language's future seems assured when so many organizations come to have a vested interest in it.

Origins

How far back do we have to go in order to find the origins of global English? In a sense, the language has always been on the move. As soon as it arrived in England from northern Europe, in the fifth century, it began to spread around the British Isles. It entered parts of Wales, Cornwall, Cumbria and southern Scotland, traditionally the strongholds of the Celtic languages. After the Norman invasion of 1066, many nobles from England fled north to Scotland, where they were made welcome, and eventually the language (in a distinctive Scots variety) spread throughout the Scottish lowlands. From the twelfth century, Anglo-Norman knights were sent across the Irish Sea, and Ireland gradually fell under English rule.[1]

But, compared with later events, these were movements on a very local scale – within the British Isles. The first significant step in the progress of English towards its status as a global language did not take place for another 300 years, towards the end of the sixteenth century. At that time, the number of mother-tongue English speakers in the world is thought to have been between 5 and 7 million, almost all of them living in the British Isles. Between the end of the reign of Elizabeth I (1603) and the beginning of the reign of Elizabeth II (1952), this figure increased almost fiftyfold, to some 250 million, the vast majority living outside the British

[1] For a fuller account of these early movements, see Crystal (1995a: Part 1). See this source also for fuller accounts of the regions described throughout this chapter.

Isles. Most of these people were, and continue to be, Americans, and it is in sixteenth-century North America that we first find a fresh dimension being added to the history of the language.

America

The first expedition from England to the New World was commissioned by Walter Raleigh in 1584, and proved to be a failure. A group of explorers landed near Roanoke Island, in what is now North Carolina, and established a small settlement. Conflict with the native people followed, and it proved necessary for a ship to return to England for help and supplies. By the time these arrived, in 1590, none of the original group of settlers could be found. The mystery of their disappearance has never been solved.

The first permanent English settlement dates from 1607, when an expedition arrived in Chesapeake Bay. The colonists called their settlement Jamestown (after James I) and the area Virginia (after the 'Virgin Queen', Elizabeth). Further settlements quickly followed along the coast, and also on the nearby islands, such as Bermuda. Then, in November 1620, the first group of Puritans, thirty-five members of the English Separatist Church, arrived on the *Mayflower* in the company of sixty-seven other settlers. Prevented by storms from reaching Virginia, they landed at Cape Cod Bay, and established a settlement at what is now Plymouth, Massachusetts.

The group was extremely mixed, ranging in age from young children to people in their 50s, and with diverse regional, social, and occupational backgrounds. What the 'Pilgrim Fathers' (as they were later called) had in common was their search for a land where they could found a new religious kingdom, free from persecution and 'purified' from the church practices they had experienced in England. It was a successful settlement, and by 1640 about 25,000 immigrants had come to the area.

The two settlements – one in Virginia, to the south, the other to the north, in present-day New England – had different linguistic backgrounds. Although the southern colony brought settlers from several parts of England, many of them came from England's 'West Country' – such counties as Somerset and

31

Early English-speaking settlement areas in America

Gloucestershire – and brought with them its characteristic accent, with its 'Zummerzet' voicing of *s* sounds, and the *r* strongly pronounced after vowels. Echoes of this accent can still be heard in the speech of communities living in some of the isolated valleys and islands in the area, such as Tangier Island in Chesapeake Bay. These 'Tidewater' accents, as they are called, have changed somewhat over the past 300 years, but not as rapidly (because of the relative isolation of the speakers) as elsewhere in the country.

By contrast, many of the Plymouth colonists came from counties in the east of England – in particular, Lincolnshire, Nottinghamshire, Essex, Kent and London, with some from the Midlands, and a few from further afield. These eastern accents were rather different – notably, lacking an *r* after vowels – and they proved to be the dominant influence in this area. The tendency 'not to pronounce the *r* is still a feature of the speech of people from New England.

The later population movements across America largely preserved the dialect distinctions which arose out of these early patterns of settlement. The New England people moved west into the region of the Great Lakes; the southerners moved along the Gulf Coast and into Texas; and the midlanders spread throughout the whole of the vast, mid-western area, across the Mississippi and ultimately into California.[2] The dialect picture was never a neat one, because of widespread north–south movements within the country, and the continuing inflow of immigrants from different parts of the world. There are many mixed dialect areas, and pockets of unexpected dialect forms. But the main divisions of north, midland, and south are still found throughout America today.

During the seventeenth century, new shiploads of immigrants brought an increasing variety of linguistic backgrounds into the country. Pennsylvania, for example, came to be settled mainly by Quakers whose origins were mostly in the Midlands and the north of England. People speaking very different kinds of English thus found themselves living alongside each other, as the 'middle' Atlantic areas (New York, in particular) became the focus of settlement. As a result, the sharp divisions between regional dialects gradually began to blur.

Then, in the eighteenth century, there was a vast wave of immigration from northern Ireland. The Irish had been migrating to America from around 1600, but the main movements took place during the 1720s, when around 50,000 Irish and Scots-Irish immigrants arrived. By the time independence was declared (1776), it is thought that one in seven of the colonial population was Scots-Irish. Many stayed along the coast, especially in the area of Philadelphia, but most moved inland through the mountains in search of land. They were seen as frontier people, with an accent which at the time was described as 'broad'. The opening up of the south and west was largely due to the pioneering spirit of this group of settlers.

---

[2] For US dialects see Williamson and Burke (1971). The displacement of the Amerindian populations, and the tragic consequences for them of European immigration, are described in Crystal (2000: 72).

Major dialect areas in the USA: Northern, Midland, Southern

By the time of the first census, in 1790, the population of the country was around 4 million, most of whom lived along the Atlantic coast. A century later, after the opening up of the west, the population numbered over 50 million, spread throughout the continent. The accent which emerged can now be heard all over the so-called Sunbelt (from Virginia to southern California), and is the accent most commonly associated with present-day American speech.

It was not only England which influenced the directions that the English language was to take in America, and later the USA. The Spanish had occupied large parts of the west and south-west. The French were present in the northern territories, around the St Lawrence River, and throughout the middle regions (French Louisiana) as far as the Gulf of Mexico. The Dutch were in New York (originally New Amsterdam) and the surrounding area. Large numbers of Germans began to arrive at the end of the seventeenth century, settling mainly in Pennsylvania and its hinterland. In addition, there were increasing numbers of Africans entering the south, as a result of the slave trade, and this dramatically increased in the eighteenth century: a population of little more than 2,500 black slaves in 1700 had become about 100,000 by 1775, far out-numbering the southern whites.

The nineteenth century saw a massive increase in American immigration, as people fled the results of revolution, poverty, and famine in Europe. Large numbers of Irish came following the potato famine in Ireland in the 1840s. Germans and Italians came, escaping the consequences of the failed 1848 revolutions. And, as the century wore on, there were increasing numbers of Central European Jews, especially fleeing from the pogroms of the 1880s. In the first two decades of the twentieth century, immigrants were entering the USA at an average of three-quarters of a million a year. In 1900, the population was just over 75 million. This total had doubled by 1950.

Within one or two generations of arrival, most of these immigrant families had come to speak English, through a natural process of assimilation. Grandparents and grandchildren found themselves living in very different linguistic worlds. The result was a massive growth in mother-tongue use of English.

According to the 1990 census, the number of people (over five years of age) who spoke only English at home had grown to over 198 million – 86 per cent of the population. This figure increased to 215 million in the 2000 census (though representing a fall to 82 per cent of the population). This is almost four times as many mother-tongue speakers as any other nation.

Some commentators have suggested that the English language was a major factor in maintaining American unity throughout this period of remarkable cultural diversification – a 'glue' which brought people together and a medium which gave them common access to opportunity.[3] At the same time, some minority groups began to be concerned about the preservation of their cultural and linguistic heritage, within a society which was becoming increasingly monolingual. The seeds of a conflict between the need for intelligibility and the need for identity were beginning to grow – a conflict which, by the later decades of the twentieth century, had fuelled the movement in support of English as the official language of the USA (see chapter 5).

Canada

Meanwhile, the English language was making progress further north. The first English-language contact with Canada was as early as 1497, when John Cabot is thought to have reached Newfoundland; but English migration along the Atlantic coast did not develop until a century later, when the farming, fishing, and fur-trading industries attracted English-speaking settlers. There was ongoing conflict with the French, whose presence dated from the explorations of Jacques Cartier in the 1520s; but this came to an end when the French claims were gradually surrendered during the eighteenth century, following their defeat in Queen Anne's War (1702–13) and the French and Indian War (1754–63). During the 1750s thousands of French settlers were deported from Acadia (modern Nova Scotia), and were replaced by settlers from New England. The numbers were then further increased by many coming directly from England, Ireland, and Scotland

---

[3] For a discussion of the issues, see Herriman and Burnaby (1996: chapter 6), and also chapter 5 below.

The movement of English into Canada

(whose earlier interest in the country is reflected in the name *Nova Scotia* 'New Scotland').

The next major development followed the US Declaration of Independence in 1776. Loyalist supporters of Britain (the 'United Empire Loyalists') found themselves unable to stay in the new United States, and most left for Canada, settling first in what is now Nova Scotia, then moving to New Brunswick and further inland. They were soon followed by many thousands (the so-called 'late Loyalists') who were attracted by the cheapness of land, especially in the area known as Upper Canada (above Montreal and north of the Great Lakes). Within fifty years, the population of this province had reached 100,000. Over 31 million were estimated in 2001, with two-thirds claiming English as a native or home language.

Because of its origins, Canadian English has a great deal in common with the rest of the English spoken in North America,

The Caribbean Islands, showing (a) countries where Standard English is an official language; in these areas, English-based creoles are also widely used; (b) countries where a language other than English is the official language, but an English-based creole is none the less spoken. The special standing of US English in Puerto Rico in Duarte Rico is noted but.

and those who live outside Canada often find it difficult to hear the difference. Many British people identify a Canadian accent as American; many Americans identify it as British. Canadians themselves insist on not being identified with either group, and certainly the variety does display a number of unique features. In addition, the presence of French as a co-official language, chiefly spoken in Quebec, produces a sociolinguistic situation not found in other English-speaking countries.[4]

The Caribbean

During the early years of American settlement, the English language was also spreading in the south. A highly distinctive kind of speech was emerging in the islands of the West Indies and the southern part of the mainland, spoken by the incoming black population. This was a consequence of the importation of African slaves to work on the sugar plantations, a practice started by the Spanish as early as 1517.

From the early seventeenth century, ships from Europe travelled to the West African coast, where they exchanged cheap goods for black slaves. The slaves were shipped in barbarous conditions to the Caribbean islands and the American coast, where they were in turn exchanged for such commodities as sugar, rum, and molasses. The ships then returned to England, completing an 'Atlantic triangle' of journeys, and the process began again. The first twenty African slaves arrived in Virginia on a Dutch ship in 1619. By the time of the American Revolution (1776) their numbers had grown to half a million, and there were over 4 million by the time slavery was abolished, at the end of the US Civil War (1865).

The policy of the slave-traders was to bring people of different language backgrounds together in the ships, to make it difficult for groups to plot rebellion. The result was the growth of several pidgin forms of communication, and in particular a pidgin between the slaves and the sailors, many of whom spoke English.

[4] For the sociolinguistic situation in contemporary Canada, see Herriman and Burnaby (1996: chapter 7).

Once arrived in the Caribbean, this pidgin English continued to act as a means of communication between the black population and the new landowners, and among the blacks themselves. Then, when their children were born, the pidgin gradually began to be used as a mother tongue, producing the first black creole speech in the region.

It is this creole English which rapidly came to be used throughout the southern plantations, and in many of the coastal towns and islands. At the same time, standard British English was becoming a prestige variety throughout the area, because of the emerging political influence of Britain. Creole forms of French, Spanish and Portuguese were also developing in and around the Caribbean, and some of these interacted with both the creole and the standard varieties of English. The Caribbean islands, and parts of the adjacent Central and South American mainland, thus came to develop a remarkably diverse range of varieties of English, reflecting their individual political and cultural histories.[5] Moreover, West Indian speech did not stay within the Caribbean islands, but moved well outside, with large communities eventually found in Canada, the USA and Britain.

Australia and New Zealand

Towards the end of the eighteenth century, the continuing process of British world exploration established the English language in the southern hemisphere. The numbers of speakers have never been very large, by comparison with those in the northern hemisphere, but the varieties of English which have emerged are just as distinctive.

Australia was visited by James Cook in 1770, and within twenty years Britain had established its first penal colony at Sydney, thus relieving the pressure on the overcrowded prisons in England. About 130,000 prisoners were transported during the fifty years after the arrival of the 'first fleet' in 1788. 'Free' settlers, as they

---

[5] For a review of issues relating to African-American English, see Harrison and Trabasso (1976). For West Indian speech in Britain, see Sutcliffe (1982).

were called, also began to enter the country from the very beginning, but they did not achieve substantial numbers until the
mid-nineteenth century. From then on, immigration rapidly increased. By 1850, the population of Australia was about 400,000,
and by 1900 nearly 4 million. In 2002, it was nearly 19 million.
The British Isles provided the main source of settlers, and thus
the main influence on the language. Many of the convicts came
from London and Ireland (especially following the 1798 Irish
rebellion), and features of the Cockney accent of London and
the brogue of Irish English can be traced in the speech patterns
heard in Australia today. On the other hand, the variety contains
many expressions which have originated in Australia (including a
number from Aboriginal languages), and in recent years the influence of American English and of a growing number of immigrant
groups has been noticeable, so that the country now has a very
mixed linguistic character.[6]

In New Zealand (whose Maori name is *Aotearoa*), the story
of English started later and moved more slowly. Captain Cook
charted the islands in 1769–70, and European whalers and traders
began to settle there in the 1790s, expanding the developments
already taking place in Australia. Christian missionary work began
among the Maori from about 1814. However, the official colony
was not established until 1840, following the Treaty of Waitangi
between Maori chiefs and the British Crown. There was then a
rapid increase in European immigration – from around 2,000 in
1840 to 25,000 by 1850, and to three-quarters of a million by
1900. As early as the turn of the century visitors to the country were making comments on the emergence of a New Zealand
accent. The total population in 2002 was over 3.8 million.

Three strands of New Zealand's social history in the present
century have had especial linguistic consequences. Firstly, in comparison with Australia, there has been a stronger sense of the historical relationship with Britain, and a greater sympathy for British
values and institutions. Many people speak with an accent which

---

[6] For the sociolinguistic situation in contemporary Australia and New
Zealand, see Herriman and Burnaby (1996: chapters 3–4), Burridge and
Mulder (1998).

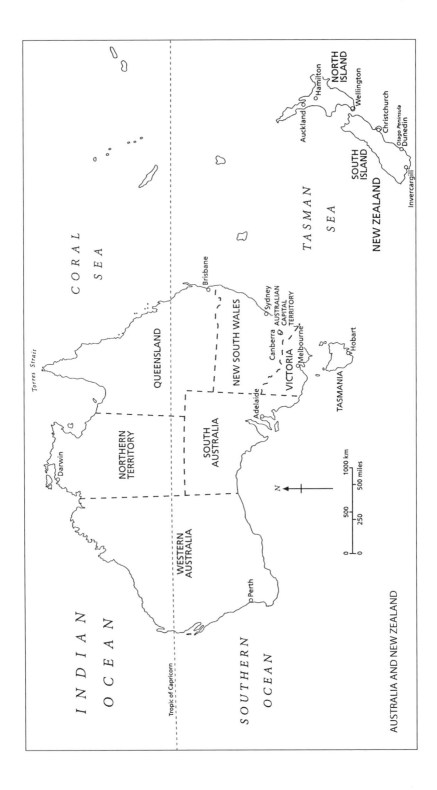

AUSTRALIA AND NEW ZEALAND

displays clear British influence. Secondly, there has been a growing sense of national identity, and in particular an emphasis on the differences between New Zealand and Australia. This has drawn attention to differences in the accents of the two countries, and motivated the use of distinctive New Zealand vocabulary. Thirdly, there has been a fresh concern to take account of the rights and needs of the Maori people, who now form over 10 per cent of the population. This has resulted in an increased use of Maori words in New Zealand English.

South Africa

Although Dutch colonists arrived in the Cape as early as 1652, British involvement in the region dates only from 1795, during the Napoleonic Wars, when an expeditionary force invaded. British control was established in 1806, and a policy of settlement began in earnest in 1820, when some 5,000 British were given land in the eastern Cape. English was made the official language of the region in 1822, and there was an attempt to anglicize the large Afrikaans-speaking population. English became the language of law, education, and most other aspects of public life. Further British settlements followed in the 1840s and 1850s, especially in Natal, and there was a massive influx of Europeans following the development of the gold and diamond areas in the Witwatersrand in the 1870s. Nearly half a million immigrants, many of them English-speaking, arrived in the country during the last quarter of the nineteenth century.

The English language history of the region thus has many strands. There was initially a certain amount of regional dialect variation among the different groups of British settlers, with the speech of the London area prominent in the Cape, and Midlands and northern British speech strongly represented in Natal; but in due course a more homogeneous accent emerged – an accent that shares many similarities with the accents of Australia, which was also being settled during this period.

At the same time, English was being used as a second language by the Afrikaans speakers, and many of the Dutch colonists took this variety with them on the Great Trek of 1836, as they

South Africa, and adjacent countries

moved north to escape British rule. An African variety of English also developed, spoken by the black population, who had learned the language mainly in mission schools, and which was influenced in different ways by the various language backgrounds of the speakers. In addition, English came to be used, along with Afrikaans and often other languages, by those with an ethnically mixed background ('coloureds'); and it was also adopted by the many immigrants from India, who were brought to the country from around 1860.

English has always been a minority language in South Africa, and is currently spoken as a first language only by about 3.7 million in a 2002 population of over 43.5 million. Afrikaans, which was given official status in 1925, was the first language of the majority of whites, including most of those in power, and acted as an important symbol of identity for those of Afrikaner background. It was also the first language of most of the coloured population. English was used by the remaining whites (of British background) and by increasing numbers of the (70 per cent majority) black population. There is thus a linguistic side to the political divisions which marked South African apartheid society: Afrikaans came to be perceived by the black majority as the language of authority and repression; English was perceived by the Afrikaner government as the language of protest and self-determination. Many blacks saw English as a means of achieving an international voice, and uniting themselves with other black communities.

On the other hand, the contemporary situation regarding the use of English is more complex than any simple opposition suggests. For the white authorities, too, English is important as a means of international communication, and 'upwardly mobile' Afrikaners have become increasingly bilingual, with fluent command of an English that often resembles the British-based variety. The public statements by Afrikaner politicians in recent years, seen on world television, illustrate this ability. As a result, a continuum of accents exists, ranging from those which are strongly influenced by Afrikaans to those which are very close to British Received Pronunciation. Such complexity is inevitable in a country where the overriding issue is social and political status, and where people have striven to maintain their deeply held feelings of national and ethnic identity in the face of opposition.

The 1993 Constitution names eleven languages as official, including English and Afrikaans, in an effort to enhance the status of the country's indigenous languages. The consequences of such an ambitious multilingual policy remain to be seen, but the difficulties of administering an eleven-language formula are immense (p. 89), and it is likely that English will continue to be an important lingua franca. Enthusiasm for the language continues to grow among the black population: in 1993, for example, a series of government surveys among black parents demonstrated an overwhelming choice of English as the preferred language in which children should receive their education. And in the South African Parliament in 1994 the language continued to dominate the proceedings, with 87 per cent of all speeches being made in English.[7]

South Asia

In terms of numbers of English speakers, the Indian subcontinent has a very special position, probably outranking the combined totals of speakers in the USA and UK. This is largely due to the special position which the language has come to hold in India itself, where estimates have been undergoing radical revision in recent years. The traditional view[8] was that somewhere between 3 and 5 per cent of the people made regular use of English, which would have yielded a total of some 30–50 million around the year 1999, when the population of India passed a billion. Since then, the estimates have crept up – nearly 20 per cent, for example, in one encyclopedia summary.[9] But some surveys have suggested much larger totals, if a flexible notion of fluency is permitted (see p. 68), with one influential review estimating that perhaps a third of the people of India are now capable of holding a conversation

---

[7] For the sociolinguistic situation in contemporary South Africa, see Herriman and Burnaby (1996: chapter 2).
[8] A figure of 3%, for example, is a widely quoted estimate of the mid-1980s (e.g. Kachru (1986: 54)).
[9] *Encyclopaedia Britannica* (2002: 796).

in English.[10] In real terms these estimates represent a range of 30 million to over 330 million (for comprehension, with a somewhat lower figure, 200 million, for speech production – which is the figure I use in Table 1 below). And we must not forget that there are also considerable numbers of English speakers elsewhere in the region, which comprises five other countries (Bangladesh, Pakistan, Sri Lanka, Nepal, Bhutan). South Asia holds about a fifth of the world's population. Several varieties of English have emerged throughout the subcontinent, and they are sometimes collectively referred to as South Asian English. These varieties are less than 200 years old, but they are already among the most distinctive varieties in the English-speaking world.

The origins of South Asian English lie in Britain. The first regular British contact with the subcontinent came in 1600 with the formation of the British East India Company – a group of London merchants who were granted a trading monopoly in the area by Queen Elizabeth I. The Company established its first trading station at Surat in 1612, and by the end of the century others were in existence at Madras, Bombay and Calcutta. During the eighteenth century, it overcame competition from other European nations, especially France. As the power of the Mughal emperors declined, the Company's influence grew, and in 1765 it took over the revenue management of Bengal. Following a period of financial indiscipline among Company servants, the 1784 India Act established a Board of Control responsible to the British Parliament, and in 1858, after the Indian Mutiny, the Company was abolished and its powers handed over to the Crown.

During the period of British sovereignty (the *Raj*), from 1765 until independence in 1947, English gradually became the medium of administration and education throughout the subcontinent. The language question attracted special attention during the early nineteenth century, when colonial administrators debated the kind of educational policy which should be introduced. A recognized turning-point was Lord William Bentinck's acceptance of a Minute written by Thomas Macaulay in 1835, which proposed the introduction of an English educational system in

---

[10] A 1997 *India Today* survey reported by Kachru (2001: 411).

The countries where South Asian English is spoken

India. When the universities of Bombay, Calcutta and Madras were established in 1857, English became the primary medium of instruction, thereby guaranteeing its status and steady growth during the next century.

In India, the bitter conflict between the supporters of English, Hindi, and regional languages led in the 1960s to a 'three language formula', in which English was introduced as the chief alternative to the local state language (typically Hindi in the north and a regional language in the south). It now has the status of an 'associate' official language, with Hindi the official language. It is also recognized as the official language of four states (Manipur, Meghalaya, Nagaland, Tripura) and eight Union territories.

English has, as a consequence, retained its standing within Indian society, continuing to be used within the legal system, government administration, secondary and higher education, the armed forces, the media, business, and tourism. It is a strong unifying force. In the Dravidian-speaking areas of the south, it is widely preferred to Hindi as a lingua franca. In the north, its fortunes vary from state to state, in relation to Hindi, depending on the policies of those in power. In Pakistan, it is an associated official language. It has no official status in the other countries of South Asia, but throughout the region it is universally used as the medium of international communication. Increasingly it is being perceived by young South Asians as the language of cultural modernity.

Former colonial Africa

Despite several centuries of European trade with African nations, by the end of the eighteenth century only the Dutch at the Cape had established a permanent settlement. However, by 1914 colonial ambitions on the part of Britain, France, Germany, Portugal, Italy and Belgium had resulted in the whole continent (apart from Liberia and Ethiopia) being divided into colonial territories. After the two World Wars there was a repartitioning of the region, with the confiscation of German and Italian territories. Most of the countries created by this partition achieved independence in or after the 1960s, and the Organization of African Unity pledged itself to maintain existing boundaries.

The English began to visit West Africa from the end of the fifteenth century, and soon after we find sporadic references to the use of the language as a lingua franca in some coastal settlements. By the beginning of the nineteenth century, the increase in commerce and anti-slave-trade activities had brought English to the whole West African coast. With hundreds of local languages to contend with, a particular feature of the region was the rise of several English-based pidgins and creoles, used alongside the

The countries of West Africa

standard varieties of colonial officials, missionaries, soldiers, and traders.

British varieties developed especially in five countries, each of which now gives English official status. There was also one American influence in the region.

- **Sierra Leone** In the 1780s, philanthropists in Britain bought land to establish a settlement for freed slaves, the first groups arriving from England, Nova Scotia and Jamaica. The settlement became a Crown Colony in 1808, and was then used as a base for anti-slave-trading squadrons, whose operations eventually brought some 60,000 'recaptives' to the country. The chief form of communication was an English-based creole, Krio, and this rapidly spread along the West African coast. The hinterland was declared a British protectorate in 1896; and the country received its independence in 1961. Its population had grown to over 5.4 million by 2002, most of whom can use Krio.

- **Ghana** (formerly **Gold Coast**) Following a successful British expedition against the Ashanti to protect trading interests, the southern Gold Coast was declared a Crown Colony in 1874. The modern state was created in 1957 by the union of this colony and the adjacent British Togoland trust territory, which had been mandated to Britain after World War I. Ghana achieved independence in 1957. Its population was nearly 19 million in 2002, about 1.5 million of whom use English as a second language.

- **Gambia** English trading along the Gambia River dates from the early seventeenth century. A period of conflict with France was followed in 1816 by the establishment of Bathurst (modern Banjul) as a British base for anti-slaver activities. The capital became a Crown Colony in 1843, the country an independent member of the Commonwealth in 1965 and a republic in 1970. It had a population of 1.4 million in 2002. Krio is widely used as a lingua franca.

- **Nigeria** After a period of early nineteenth-century British exploration of the interior, a British colony was founded at Lagos in 1861. This amalgamated with other southern and northern territories to form a single country in 1914, and it received

51

independence in 1960. It is one of the most multilingual countries in Africa, with some 500 languages identified in the mid-1990s. Its population in 2002 was over 126 million. About half use pidgin or creole English as a second language.

- **Cameroon** Explored by the Portuguese, Spanish, Dutch and British, this region became a German protectorate in 1884, and was divided between France and Britain in 1919. After some uncertainty, the two areas merged as a single country in 1972, with both French and English remaining as official languages. It is also a highly multilingual region, with a 2002 population of nearly 16 million. It is thus a country in which contact languages have flourished, notably Cameroon Pidgin, spoken by about half the population.

- **Liberia** Africa's oldest republic was founded in 1822 through the activities of the American Colonization Society, which wished to establish a homeland for former slaves. Within fifty years it received some 13,000 black Americans, as well as some 6,000 slaves recaptured at sea. The settlement became a republic in 1847, and adopted a constitution based on that of the USA. It managed to retain its independence despite pressure from European countries during the nineteenth-century 'scramble for Africa'. Its population in 2002 was some 3.2 million, most of whom use pidgin English as a second language (but there are also a number of first-language speakers). Links with US African-American English are still very evident.

Although English ships had visited East Africa from the end of the sixteenth century, systematic interest began only in the 1850s, with the expeditions to the interior of such British explorers as Richard Burton, David Livingstone and John Speke. The Imperial British East Africa Company was founded in 1888, and soon afterwards a system of colonial protectorates became established, while other European nations (Germany, France, and Italy) vied with Britain for territorial control.

Several modern states, each with a history of association with Britain, gave English official status when they gained independence, and British English has thus played a major role in the development of these states, being widely used in government, the courts, schools, the media, and other public domains. It has also been adopted elsewhere in the region as a medium of international communication, such as in Rwanda, Ethiopia and Somalia.

- **Botswana** Under British protection from 1885, the southern part of the country became part of Cape Colony in 1895, the northern part becoming Bechuanaland. It received its independence in 1966. Population in 2002 was 1.5 million. English is the official language.
- **Kenya** A British colony from 1920, this country became independent in 1963, following a decade of unrest (the Mau Mau rebellion). English was then made the official language, with Swahili made a national language in 1974. English none the less retains an important role in the country, which had some 31 million people in 2002.
- **Lesotho** Under British protection as Basutoland from 1869, it became independent in 1960. Its population was nearly 2.2 million in 2002. English is the official language.
- **Malawi** (formerly **Nyasaland**) The area became a British colony in 1907, and received its independence in 1964. Its population was 10.5 million in 2002. English is an official language along with Chewa.
- **Namibia** A German protectorate from 1884, it was mandated to South Africa – by the League of Nations in 1920 – who later annexed it (as South-West Africa). The United Nations assumed direct responsibility in 1966, and the country became known as Namibia, receiving full independence in 1990. Its population in 2002 was 1.8 million. English is the official language.
- **Tanzania** (formerly **Zanzibar** and **Tanganyika**) Zanzibar became a British protectorate in 1890, and Britain received a mandate for Tanganyika in 1919. The first East African country to gain independence (1961), its population was over 36 million in 2002. English was a joint official language with Swahili until 1967, then lost its status as a national language; but it remains an important medium of communication.
- **Uganda** The Uganda kingdoms were united as a British protectorate between 1893 and 1903, and the country received its

independence in 1962. Its population was over 24 million in 2002. English is the sole official language, but Swahili is also widely used as a lingua franca.

- **Zambia** (formerly **Northern Rhodesia**) At first administered by the British South Africa Company, the country became a British protectorate in 1924, and received its independence in 1964. Its population was over 11 million in 2002. English is the official language.
- **Zimbabwe** (formerly **Southern Rhodesia**) Also administered by the British South Africa Company, it became a British colony in 1923. Opposition to independence under African rule led to a Unilateral Declaration of Independence (UDI) by the white-dominated government in 1965. Power was eventually transferred to the African majority, and the country achieved its independence in 1980. Its population was around 11 million in 2002. English is the official language.

The kinds of English which developed in East Africa were very different from those found in West Africa. Large numbers of British emigrants settled in the area, producing a class of expatriates and African-born whites (farmers, doctors, university lecturers, etc.) which never emerged in the environmentally less hospitable West African territories. A British model was introduced early on into schools, reinforcing the exposure to British English brought by the many missionary groups around the turn of the century. The result was a range of mother-tongue English varieties which have more in common with what is heard in South Africa or Australia than in Nigeria or Ghana.[11]

South-east Asia and the South Pacific

The territories in and to the west of the South Pacific display an interesting mixture of American and British English. The main American presence emerged after the Spanish-American War of 1898, from which the USA received the island of Guam

---

[11] For the sociolinguistic situation in contemporary West and East Africa, see Bamgbose (2000).

The countries of East and Southern Africa

(and Puerto Rico in the Caribbean) and sovereignty over the Philippines. Hawaii was annexed at that time also, after a period of increasing US influence. In the 1940s, the US invasion of Japanese-held Pacific islands was followed after World War II by several areas being made the responsibility of the USA as United Nations Trust Territories. The Philippines became independent in 1946, but the influence of American English remains strong. And as this country has by far the largest population of the English-speaking states in the region (about 80 million in 2002), it makes a significant contribution to world totals.

British influence began through the voyages of English sailors at the end of the eighteenth century, notably the journeys of Captain Cook in the 1770s. The London Missionary Society sent its workers to the islands of the South Pacific fifty years later. In South-east Asia, the development of a British colonial empire grew from the work of Stamford Raffles, an administrator in the British East India Company. Centres were established in several locations, notably Penang (1786), Singapore (1819) and Malacca (1824). Within a few months, the population of Singapore had grown to over 5,000, and by the time the Federated Malay States were brought together as a Crown Colony (1867), English had come to be established throughout the region as the medium of law and administration, and was being increasingly used in other contexts. A famous example is the English-language daily newspaper, *The Straits Times*, which began publication in 1845.

English inevitably and rapidly became the language of power in the British territories of South-east Asia. Hong Kong island was ceded to Britain in 1842 by the Treaty of Nanking, at the end of the first Opium War, and Kowloon was added to it in 1860; the New Territories, which form the largest part of the colony, were leased from China in 1898 for ninety-nine years. Towards the end of the nineteenth century, several territories in the region became British protectorates, the administration of some being later taken over by Australia and New Zealand. Territories with English as part of their heritage, which have become independent in recent decades, include American Samoa, Palau (Belau), Fiji, Kiribati, Marshall Islands, Federated States of Micronesia, North Mariana Islands, Samoa, Tonga, Tuvalu, and Vanuatu.

The introduction of a British educational system exposed learners to a standard British English model very early on. English-medium schools began in Penang (now Malaysia's leading port) in 1816, with senior teaching staff routinely brought in from Britain. Although at the outset these schools were attended by only a tiny percentage of the population, numbers increased during the nineteenth century as waves of Chinese and Indian immigrants entered the area. English rapidly became the language of professional advancement and the chief literary language. Soon after the turn of the century, higher education through the medium of English was also introduced. The language thus became a prestige lingua franca among those who had received an English education and who had thereby entered professional society.

Despite the common colonial history of the region, a single variety of 'South-east Asian English' has not emerged. The political histories of Singapore and Malaysia, especially since independence, have been too divergent for this to happen; and the sociolinguistic situations in Hong Kong and Papua New Guinea are unique.[12]

- **Singapore** In the 1950s a bilingual educational system was introduced in Singapore, with English used as a unifying medium alongside Chinese, Malay, and Tamil. However, English remained the language of government and the legal system, and retained its importance in education and the media. Its use has also been steadily increasing among the general population. In a 1975 survey, only 27 per cent of people over age forty claimed to understand English, whereas among fifteen- to twenty-year-olds, the proportion was over 87 per cent. There is also evidence of quite widespread use in family settings, and a new local variety, known as Singlish, has evolved (p. 174). The country had a population of around 4.3 million in 2002.
- **Malaysia** The situation is very different in Malaysia where, following independence (1957), Bahasa Malaysia was adopted as the national language, and the role of English accordingly became more restricted. Malay-medium education was introduced, with English an obligatory subject but increasingly being seen as of value for international rather than intra-national purposes – more a foreign language than a second language.

---

[12] For the sociolinguistic situation in South-east Asia, see: for Hong Kong, Li (1999), Evans and Green (2001); for Malaysia, Said and Siew (2000); for the Philippines, Bautista (1997); for Singapore, Gopinathan, Pakir, Kam and Saravanan (1998).

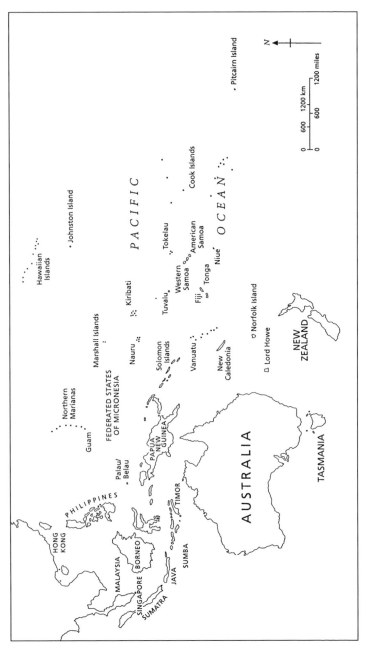

The location of territories in South-east Asia and the South Pacific

However, the traditional prestige attached to English still exists, for many speakers. The country had a population of over 22 million in 2002.

- **Hong Kong** English has always had a limited use in the territory, associated with government or military administration, law, business, and the media. Chinese (Cantonese) is the mother-tongue of over 98 per cent of the population (over 7 million in 2002). However, in recent years there has been a major increase in educational provision, with estimates suggesting that over a quarter of the population have some competence in English. English and Chinese have joint official status, but Chinese predominates in most speech situations, often with a great deal of language mixing. There is uncertainty surrounding the future role of English, following the 1997 transfer of power, though patterns of language use so far have shown little change.

- **Papua New Guinea** British sailors visited the territory as early as 1793, and Britain and Germany annexed areas in 1884. British New Guinea was transferred to Australia in 1904 as the Territory of Papua; German New Guinea was mandated to Australia in 1921. The two areas merged after World War 2, and became independent in 1975. There was a population of nearly 5 million in 2002. About half the people speak Tok Pisin, an English-based pidgin, as a second language (and some have it as a mother tongue). It has a nation-wide presence, widely seen in advertisements and the press, and heard on radio and television. Many major works have been translated into Tok Pisin, including Shakespeare and the Bible.

A world view

The present-day world status of English is primarily the result of two factors: the expansion of British colonial power, which peaked towards the end of the nineteenth century, and the emergence of the United States as the leading economic power of the twentieth century. It is the latter factor which continues to explain the world position of the English language today (much to the discomfiture of some in Britain who find the loss of historical linguistic pre-eminence unpalatable). The USA has nearly 70 per cent of all English mother-tongue speakers in the world (excluding creole varieties). Such dominance, with its political/economic under-pinnings, currently gives America a controlling interest in the way the language is likely to develop.

How then may we summarize this complex situation? The US linguist Braj Kachru has suggested that we think of the spread of English around the world as three concentric circles, representing different ways in which the language has been acquired and is currently used.[13] Although not all countries fit neatly into this model, it has been widely regarded as a helpful approach.

- The *inner circle* refers to the traditional bases of English, where it is the primary language: it includes the USA, UK, Ireland, Canada, Australia and New Zealand.

- The *outer* or *extended circle* involves the earlier phases of the spread of English in non-native settings, where the language has become part of a country's chief institutions, and plays an important 'second language' role in a multilingual setting: it includes Singapore, India, Malawi and over fifty other territories.

- The *expanding* or *extending circle* involves those nations which recognize the importance of English as an international language, though they do not have a history of colonization by members of the inner circle, nor have they given English any special administrative status. It includes China, Japan, Greece, Poland and (as the name of this circle suggests) a steadily in-creasing number of other states. In these areas, English is taught as a foreign language. (The term 'expanding' reflects its origins in the 1980s: today, with English recognized virtually every-where, a tense change to *expanded circle* would better reflect the contemporary scene.)

There are some seventy-five territories in which English has held or continues to hold a special place, as a member of either the inner or the outer circles. These are given in a single alphabetical list

---

[13] For example, in Kachru (1988: 5).

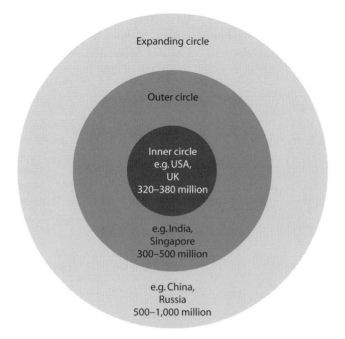

The three 'circles' of English

below (Table 1), along with an estimate of the number of speakers. The national population figures are estimates for 2001. L1 stands for people who have a variety of English as a first language, or mother tongue. L2 stands for people who have learned a variety of English as a second language, in addition to their mother tongue. Where I have been unable to find any relevant data, the figure for L1 or L2 is missing.

Lists of this kind contain all kinds of hidden assumptions, and they have to be carefully interpreted. In particular, we should note the following points:

- There is no single source of statistical information on language totals, so estimates have to be taken from a variety of sources. In the first instance, I used the latest editions of the *UNESCO statistical yearbook*, *The Encyclopaedia Britannica yearbook*, and *Ethnologue: languages of the world*, and whatever census data I

Table 1 *Speakers of English in territories where the language has had special relevance*

Territory	Population (2001)	Usage estimate	
American Samoa	67,000	L1	2,000
		L2	65,000
Antigua & Barbuda (c)	68,000	L1	66,000
		L2	2,000
Aruba	70,000	L1	9,000
		L2	35,000
Australia	18,972,000	L1	14,987,000
		L2	3,500,000
Bahamas (c)	298,000	L1	260,000
		L2	28,000
Bangladesh	131,270,000	L2	3,500,000
Barbados (c)	275,000	L1	262,000
		L2	13,000
Belize (c)	256,000	L1	190,000
		L2	56,000
Bermuda	63,000	L1	63,000
Botswana	1,586,000	L2	630,000
British Virgin Islands (c)	20,800	L1	20,000
Brunei	344,000	L1	10,000
		L2	134,000
Cameroon (c)	15,900,000	L2	7,700,000
Canada	31,600,000	L1	20,000,000
		L2	7,000,000
Cayman Islands (c)	36,000	L1	36,000
Cook Islands	21,000	L1	1,000
		L2	3,000
Dominica (c)	70,000	L1	3,000
		L2	60,000
Fiji	850,000	L1	6,000
		L2	170,000
Gambia (c)	1,411,000	L2	40,000
Ghana (c)	19,894,000	L2	1,400,000
Gibraltar	31,000	L1	28,000
		L2	2,000
Grenada (c)	100,000	L1	100,000

Table 1 (*cont.*)

Territory	Population (2001)	Usage estimate	
Guam	160,000	L1	58,000
		L2	100,000
Guyana (c)	700,000	L1	650,000
		L2	30,000
Hong Kong	7,210,000	L1	150,000
		L2	2,200,000
India	1,029,991,000	L1	350,000
		L2	200,000,000
Ireland	3,850,000	L1	3,750,000
		L2	100,000
Jamaica (c)	2,665,000	L1	2,600,000
		L2	50,000
Kenya	30,766,000	L2	2,700,000
Kiribati	94,000	L2	23,000
Lesotho	2,177,000	L2	500,000
Liberia (c)	3,226,000	L1	600,000
		L2	2,500,000
Malawi	10,548,000	L2	540,000
Malaysia	22,230,000	L1	380,000
		L2	7,000,000
Malta	395,000	L1	13,000
		L2	95,000
Marshall Islands	70,000	L2	60,000
Mauritius	1,190,000	L1	2,000
		L2	200,000
Micronesia	135,000	L1	4,000
		L2	60,000
Montserrat (c)	4,000	L1	4,000
Nambia	1,800,000	L1	14,000
		L2	300,000
Nauru	12,000	L1	900
		L2	10,700
Nepal	25,300,000	L2	7,000,000
New Zealand	3,864,000	L1	3,700,000
		L2	150,000

(*cont.*)

Table 1 (*cont.*)

Territory	Population (2001)	Usage estimate	
Nigeria (c)	126,636,000	L2	60,000,000
Northern Marianas (c)	75,000	L1	5,000
		L2	65,000
Pakistan	145,000,000	L2	17,000,000
Palau	19,000	L1	500
		L2	18,000
Papua New Guinea (c)	5,000,000	L1	150,000
		L2	3,000,000
Philippines	83,000,000	L1	20,000
		L2	40,000,000
Puerto Rico	3,937,000	L1	100,000
		L2	1,840,000
Rwanda	7,313,000	L2	20,000
St Kitts & Nevis (c)	43,000	L1	43,000
St Lucia (c)	158,000	L1	31,000
		L2	40,000
St Vincent & Grenadines (c)	116,000	L1	114,000
Samoa	180,000	L1	1,000
		L2	93,000
Seychelles	80,000	L1	3,000
		L2	30,000
Sierra Leone (c)	5,427,000	L1	500,000
		L2	4,400,000
Singapore	4,300,000	L1	350,000
		L2	2,000,000
Solomon Islands (c)	480,000	L1	10,000
		L2	165,000
South Africa	43,586,000	L1	3,700,000
		L2	11,000,000
Sri Lanka	19,400,000	L1	10,000
		L2	1,900,000
Suriname (c)	434,000	L1	260,000
		L2	150,000
Swaziland	1,104,000	L2	50,000
Tanzania	36,232,000	L2	4,000,000
Tonga	104,000	L2	30,000

Table 1 (*cont.*)

Territory	Population (2001)	Usage estimate	
Trinidad & Tobago (c)	1,170,000	L1	1,145,000
Tuvalu	11,000	L2	800
Uganda	23,986,000	L2	2,500,000
United Kingdom	59,648,000	L1	58,190,000
		L2	1,500,000
UK Islands (Channel Is, Man)	228,000	L1	227,000
United States	278,059,000	L1	215,424,000
		L2	25,600,000
US Virgin Islands (c)	122,000	L1	98,000
		L2	15,000
Vanuatu (c)	193,000	L1	60,000
		L2	120,000
Zambia	9,770,000	L1	110,000
		L2	1,800,000
Zimbabwe	11,365,000	L1	250,000
		L2	5,300,000
Other dependencies	35,000	L1	20,000
		L2	15,000
Total	2,236,730,800	L1	329,140,800
		L2	430,614,500

The category 'Other dependencies' consists of territories administered by Australia (Norfolk I., Christmas I., Cocos Is), New Zealand (Niue, Tokelau) and the UK (Anguilla, Falkland Is, Pitcairn I., Turks & Caicos Is).

could find. In a (regrettably) few cases, a sociolinguistic study of an area has provided an estimate.

• Where no linguistic estimate is available, I used an indirect method, based on the percentage of a country's population over the age of twenty-five who have completed their secondary or further education – the assumption being that, in a country where the language has official status, and is taught in schools, this figure would suggest a reasonable level of attainment.

- The notion of 'a variety of English' referred to above includes standard, pidgin, and creole varieties of English. That is why, in certain countries, the usage totals in the list are much higher than would be expected if only Standard English were being considered. In Nigeria, for example, large numbers (thought to be well over 40 per cent of the population) use Nigerian Pidgin English as a second language. The linguistic justification for this approach is that these varieties are, indeed, varieties **of English** (as opposed to, say, French), and are usually related to Standard English along a continuum. On the other hand, because the ends of this continuum may not be mutually intelligible, it could be argued that we need to keep Standard English totals separate from pidgin/creole English totals: if this view is adopted, then some 7 million L1 speakers (mainly from the Caribbean) and some 80 million L2 speakers (mainly from West Africa) should be subtracted from the grand totals. Countries where this is an issue are identified by (c) in the list.

- It is also important to recall (from chapter 1) that to have a 'special place' can mean various things. Sometimes English is an official or joint official language of a state, its status being defined by law, as in the case of India, Ireland or Canada. Sometimes it may be the sole or dominant language for historical reasons (but without official status), as in the case of the USA or the UK. In a few instances, English has lost the formal status it once had, though it still plays an important role in the community. In many cases, its standing is less certain, coexisting with other local languages in a relationship which shifts with time and social function. But in all cases, it can be argued, the population is living in an environment in which the English language is routinely in evidence, publicly accessible in varying degrees, and part of the nation's recent or present identity.

- Finally, we should bear in mind that the notion of a 'special place', as reflected in this list, is one which relates entirely to historical and political factors. This has led some linguists to argue that such a list presents a picture of the present-day world which does not wholly reflect sociolinguistic reality. In particular, it is suggested, the distinction between 'second language' (L2) and 'foreign language' use has less contemporary relevance than it formerly had. There is much more use of English nowadays in some countries of the expanding circle, where it is 'only' a foreign language (as in Scandinavia and The Netherlands), than in some of the outer circle where it has traditionally held a special place. Also, to make a language official may not mean very much, in real terms. For example, English is probably represented in Rwanda and Burundi in very comparable ways, but Rwanda is in the list (and Burundi is not) only because the former has (in 1996) made a political decision to give the language special status. What the consequences are for the future use of English in that country remains to be seen. In the meantime, it should not be forgotten that there are several countries, not represented in the Table, which are making a much more important contribution to the notion of English as a global language than is reflected by any geo-historical picture (see chapters 3 and 4).

In reflecting on these totals, we should not underestimate the significance of the overall population figure, as it indicates the total number of people who are in theory routinely exposed to English in a country. The grand total of 2,236 million in 2002 is well over a third of the world's population. But of course, only a proportion of these people actually have some command of English.

The total of 329 million represents a conservative estimate of those who have learned English as a first language (L1). The total would be increased if we knew the L1 figures for every country – especially in such areas as West Africa, where it is not known how many use a variety of English as a first language. Some reference books (such as *World almanac* and *Ethnologue)* seem to take a more inclusive stance, in this respect, citing as many as 450 million as a grand total at present. The main variable, however, is whether the various English-derived pidgins and creoles should be included under the L1 heading. If they are, a further 80 million must be added to the 329 million total – and it is this total of (approximately) 400 million which is the most commonly cited L1 total in the early 2000s.

The total of 430 million represents an estimate of those who have learned English as a second language (L2); but it does not give the whole picture. For many countries, no estimates are available. And in others (notably India, Pakistan, Nigeria, Ghana, Malaysia, Philippines and Tanzania, which had a combined total of over 1,462 million people in 2002), even a small percentage increase in the number of speakers thought to have a reasonable (rather than a fluent) command of English would considerably expand the L2 grand total. It is, in any case, now well ahead of the L1 total, whether or not pidgins and creoles are included.

No account has been taken in this list of the third category of English language learners referred to above: the members of the expanding circle, who have learned English as a foreign language. Here too, estimates for the total number of these speakers vary enormously because, as with second-language speakers, everything depends on just how great a command of English is considered acceptable to count as a 'speaker of English'. A criterion of native-speaker-like fluency would clearly produce a relatively small figure; including every beginner would produce a relatively large one. A widely circulated British Council estimate – more informed than most, as it was based on reports of numbers attending courses and taking examinations, as well as on market intelligence provided by its English 2000 project – has referred to a billion (i.e. thousand million) people engaged in learning English.[14] That figure needs to be interpreted cautiously, because it includes all learners, from beginners to advanced. If we take, as a criterion, a medium level of conversational competence in handling domestic subject-matter, then we might expect some three-quarters of this total to be counted as 'speakers of English as a foreign language' – say, 750 million. However, there need to be only small variations in percentage estimations in the more populous countries to produce a large effect on the figures. No-one knows the proficiency realities in China, for example.

Faced with such notable variations, in which people with particular political agendas can argue for English being stronger or weaker, a cautious temperament will use averages of the most

[14] British Council (1997).

recent estimates,[15] and these produce a grand total of *c.* 1,500 million speakers from all sources – approximately 750 million first- and second-language speakers, and an equivalent number of speakers of English as a foreign language. This figure permits a convenient summary, given that world population passed the 6 billion mark during late 1999. It suggests that approximately one in four of the world's population are now capable of communicating to a useful level in English.

Two comments must immediately be made about this or any similar conclusion. First, if one quarter of the world's population are able to use English, then three-quarters are not. Nor do we have to travel far into the hinterland of a country – away from the tourist spots, airports, hotels and restaurants – to encounter this reality. Populist claims about the universal spread of English thus need to be kept firmly in perspective. Second, there is evidently a major shift taking place in the centre of gravity of the language. From a time (in the 1960s) when the majority of speakers were thought to be first-language speakers, we now have a situation where there are more people speaking it as a second language, and many more speaking it as a foreign language. If we combine these two latter groups, the ratio of native to non-native is around 1:3. Moreover, the population growth in areas where English is a second language is about 2.5 times that in areas where it is a first language (see Table 2), so that this differential is steadily increasing. David Graddol suggests that the proportion of the world's population who have English as a first language will decline from over 8 per cent in 1950 to less than 5 per cent in

[15] It is interesting to compare estimates for first (L1), second (L2) and foreign (F) language use over the past 40 years.
  – in Quirk (1962: 6) the totals for first (L1), second (L2) and foreign (F) were 250 (L1) and 100 (L2/F);
  – during the 1970s these totals rose to 300 (L1), 300 (L2) and 100 (F) (cf. McArthur (1992: 355));
  – Kachru (1985: 212) has 300 (L1), 300–400 (L2) and 600–700 (F);
  – *Ethnologue* (1988) and Bright (1992: II.74), using a *Time* estimate in 1986, have 403 (L1), 397 (L2) and 800 (F);
  – during the 1990s the L1 and L2 estimates rise again, though with some variation. The *Columbia Encyclopedia* (1993) has 450 (L1), 400 and 850 (F). *Ethnologue* (1992), using a *World Almanac* estimate in 1991, has 450 (L1) and 350 (L2).

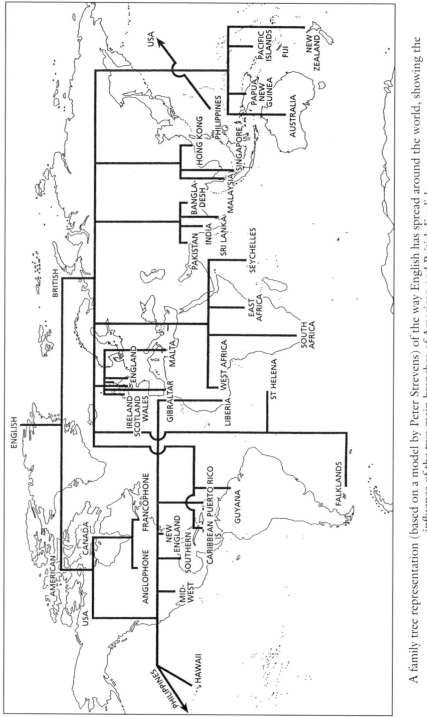

A family tree representation (based on a model by Peter Strevens) of the way English has spread around the world, showing the influence of the two main branches of American and British English

Table 2 *Annual growth rate in population in selected countries,*
*1996–2001**

	Population (2001)	% annual growth (1996–2001)
Australia	18,972,000	1.1
Canada	31,600,000	0.9
New Zealand	3,864,000	0.8
UK	59,648,000	0.4
USA	278,059,000	1.2
Average		0.88
Cameroon	15,900,000	2.6
India	1,029,991,000	1.7
Malaysia	22,229,000	2.5
Nigeria	126,636,000	2.8
Philippines	82,842,000	2.4
Average		2.4

*Population growth data from *Encyclopaedia Britannica* (2002).

2050.[16] The situation is without precedent for an international language. Much will depend on what happens in the countries with the largest populations, notably China, Japan, Russia, Indonesia and Brazil.

No other language has spread around the globe so extensively, but – as we have seen in chapter 1 – what is impressive is not so much the grand total but the speed with which expansion has taken place since the 1950s. In 1950, the case for English as a world language would have been no more than plausible. Fifty years on, and the case is virtually unassailable. What happened in this fifty years – a mere eye-blink in the history of a language – to cause such a massive change of stature? To answer this question, we must look at the way modern society has come to use, and depend on, the English language.

[16] Graddol (1999: 61).

3
Why English? The cultural foundation

———·····❧······———

'I have undertaken to write a grammar of English', says John Wallis in the preface to his *Grammar of the English language*, 'because there is clearly a great demand for it from foreigners, who want to be able to understand the various important works which are written in our tongue.' And he goes on: 'all kinds of literature are widely available in English editions, and, without boasting, it can be said that there is scarcely any worthwhile body of knowledge which has not been recorded today, adequately at least, in the English language'.[1]

This is a familiar-sounding argument to twenty-first-century ears; but these bold words are not from a modern author. John Wallis was writing in England in 1765. Moreover, the words are a translation. Wallis wrote his book in Latin, which was still being widely used as a scholarly lingua franca during the eighteenth century. But he could clearly see how the situation was changing – and had already greatly changed since the time of Shakespeare.

A few generations earlier, Richard Mulcaster, the headmaster of Merchant Taylors' School, had been one of the strongest sup-porters of the English language, avowing in 1582: 'I love Rome, but London better. I favour Italy, but England more. I honour the Latin, but I worship the English.'[2] However, Mulcaster was

---

[1] Author's preface, John Wallis, *Grammatica Linguae Anglicanae*, xxiii (Kemp (1972: 105)).
[2] Mulcaster (1582).

living in a very different intellectual climate. He felt he had to defend the language against those who believed that English should not usurp the long-established place of Latin. There were many around him who thought that a 'mere vernacular' could not be used to express great and complex thoughts. So he expressed himself strongly: 'I do not think that any language is better able to utter all arguments, either with more pith or greater plainness, as our English tongue is'. A decade later, and Shakespeare would begin to give him some evidence.

Despite his strong convictions, Mulcaster could still see that there was a problem: English was no real match for Latin at an international level. 'Our English tongue', he says at one point, 'is of small reach – it stretcheth no further than this island of ours – nay, not there over all.' He was right, for the Celtic languages were still strongly present in Britain at the time, and few people engaged in foreign travel. 'Our state', Mulcaster remarks, 'is no Empire to hope to enlarge it by commanding over countries.' But within two years, Walter Raleigh's first expedition to America had set sail, and the situation was about to alter fundamentally.

Not all were as pessimistic as Mulcaster, though. Samuel Daniel, in his poem *Musophilis*, wrote in 1599:

> And who in time knows whither we may vent
>   The treasure of our tongue, to what strange shores
> This gain of our best glory shall be sent,
> To enrich unknowing nations without stores?
> Which worlds in the yet unformed Occident
> May come refined with the accents that are ours.

Daniel's speculations did become a reality – but not for well over a century. When, fifty years later, the poet and traveller Richard Flecknoe reflected on his ten-year journey through Europe, Asia, Africa and America he found that Spanish and Dutch were the really useful languages to know, with English being only occasionally helpful – as he put it, 'to stop holes with'. But by the 1750s it was possible for the Earl of Chesterfield to write: 'I have . . . a sensible pleasure in reflecting upon the rapid progress which our language has lately made, and still continues to make, all over Europe.'[3]

[3] Chesterfield (1754).

And David Hume, writing in 1767 at a time when French was recognized as the language of international diplomacy, saw in America the key to the future success of English: 'Let the French, therefore, triumph in the present diffusion of their tongue. Our solid and increasing establishments in America . . . promise a superior stability and duration to the English language.'[4]

Many Americans agreed. In 1780 John Adams, as part of his proposal to Congress for an American Academy, was in no doubt. 'English is destined to be in the next and succeeding centuries more generally the language of the world than Latin was in the last or French is in the present age. The reason of this is obvious, because the increasing population in America, and their universal connection and correspondence with all nations will, aided by the influence of England in the world, whether great or small, force their language into general use, in spite of all the obstacles that may be thrown in their way, if any such there should be'.[5] He proved to be an accurate prophet.

We might expect that the British and Americans would themselves be loud in support of their own language. Indeed, often their views were expressed with an extravagance that we would now find embarrassing, claiming even to see divine providence in the spread of English, or suggesting that there was something intrinsically superior about its pronunciation or grammatical construction – a view which I rejected in chapter 1. It was therefore a moment of some significance when in 1851 a German, Jakob Grimm, the leading philologist of his time, commented that 'of all modern languages, not one has acquired such great strength and vigour as the English', and concluded that it 'may be called justly a language of the world . . . destined to reign in future with still more extensive sway over all parts of the globe'.[6]

His view was much quoted, and during the nineteenth century similar opinions multiplied as British imperialism grew. US linguist Richard W. Bailey, in his cultural history of the language, *Images of English*, has compiled a number of comments from contemporary

[4] Hume (1767).   [5] Adams (1780).   [6] Grimm (1851).

writers which show just how the mood had changed by the 1850s. One quotation will suffice to illustrate the prevailing opinion – from a writer in 1829:[7]

It is evident to all those who have devoted any portion of attention to the subject, that the English language would, if proper care were devoted to its advancement, stand an excellent chance of becoming more universally diffused, read, and spoken, than any other now is, or ever has been. In Europe, the study of it seems to be gradually spreading. In Germany, Russia, and Scandinavia it is esteemed an essential, in France a highly useful, branch of education; in Africa it is gradually superseding the Dutch, and becoming the medium of valuable information. In Australasia it is not only widely spoken, as the only European language known on that vast continent, but written and printed in an almost incredible number of newspapers, magazines, and reviews. In Asia so great is the desire manifested to learn it, that it was thought by Bishop Heber, that, if proper facilities were afforded, it would, in fifty years, supersede Hindoostanee, and become the court and camp language of India. In America, millions already speak, write, and read it, as their mother tongue . . . Never before did a language look forward to so bright a prospect as this . . .

And indeed, by the end of the century, as we have seen in chapter 1, English had become the language 'on which the sun never sets'.

Then, as today, some enthusiasts were moved to speculate about the world's linguistic future in ways which can best be described as fantasy. About 60 million people were speaking English around the world as a mother tongue by the 1850s – a remarkable increase indeed – but this led many writers to become very excited about the language's prospects. By the turn of the century, some calculated, there would surely be at least three times as many. And, others were predicting in the 1870s, after a further century the grand total of mother-tongue speakers would almost certainly reach 1,000 million – at least! Here is the editor of *The Phonetic Journal* (Isaac Pitman) writing about the future of English.[8] He

---

[7] Corruptions of the English language. *Gentleman's Magazine* 99 (February), 121–3. In Bailey (1991: 107).
[8] Pitman (1873: 289).

observes that the contemporary users of English number nearly 80 million, then uses formulae on population projections in various countries to reach the following conclusion:

We may estimate on this basis that in the year 2000 the most important languages will be spoken by the number of persons as under:

Italian	53,370,000
French	72,571,000
Russian	130,479,800
German	157,480,000
Spanish	505,286,242

English
Europe	178,846,153	
United States and non-European		1,837,286,53
British dependencies	1,658,440,000	

Such predictions were very wide of the mark, as we have seen in chapter 2. Even the most optimistic of estimates for mother-tongue usage in the 1990s hardly exceeded 450 million. The late nineteenth-century writers were making assumptions which were soon to prove false – that empire-building would continue at the same rate, that British industrial supremacy would be maintained, and that those who spoke minority languages would not fight back. Predicting the linguistic future is always a dangerous activity.

But the general thrust of their argument was certainly borne out, and if we include second and foreign language usage of English in the 1990s, then the prophets were more right than wrong. 'English is the language of the future', wrote William White in the weekly *The Schoolmaster* in 1872,[9] and Pitman concludes his calculations with exactly the same words. These are two out of hundreds of quotations it is possible to find in the literature of the time making this point. I have not found a single quotation to suggest that a different view was held by anyone.

[9] White (1872).

These observations reinforce the historical account given in chapter 2, illustrating the remarkably short period of time it took for English to travel around the world. But they do not give the whole story. After all, when a language arrives in a new country, it does not necessarily come to be adopted. It has to prove its worth. And there are famous occasions where the language of the new-comers does *not* end up replacing the language of the inhabitants – the most famous instance, in fact, relating to English itself, in 1066. Within 200 years of the Norman Conquest, the language of England was emerging, in the earliest Middle English literature, as – English, not French. There was no linguistic conquest. Per-haps, if the Normans had taken up residence in larger numbers, or if good political relations between England and France had lasted longer, or if English had not already been so well established since Anglo-Saxon times, the outcome might have been different. This book would then, in all probability, have been written about (and in) World French.

So what was the worth of the English language, as it grew in global stature during the nineteenth century? In which ways did people value it? In which ways have they since come to use it? In which situations do they now depend on it? The answers to these questions will give us a sense of the language's social usefulness, which is actually more informative, in addressing the question 'Why World English?' than any bare historical account of the language's geographical spread (such as the one provided in chapter 2). A geo-historical survey can help us see what happened in the past; but a socio-historical account is needed to help us explain it; and only a cultural account can give us a sense of what is likely to happen in the future.

The remainder of this chapter therefore reviews some impor-tant factors in nineteenth-century social history which laid the cultural foundation for the eventual growth of English as a world language. Then in chapter 4 I shall examine the various cultural manifestations of this development during the twentieth century which will explain the stature of the language today. We shall en-counter a series of variations on a single theme. In relation to so many of the major socio-cultural developments of the past 200 years, it can be shown that the English language has repeatedly found itself 'in the right place at the right time'.[10] No single one of these developments could have established the language as a world leader, but together they have put it in a position of pre-eminence, and together they maintain it.

Political developments

Most of the pre-twentieth-century commentators would have had no difficulty giving a single, political answer to the question 'Why World English?' They would simply have pointed to the growth of the British Empire. Isaac Pitman, for example, justifying his calculations about English as the language of the future (see p. 76), simply observes: 'The British Empire covers nearly a third of the earth's surface, and British subjects are nearly a fourth of the population of the world.'[11] It was considered self-evident that the civilizing influence of Britain was a desirable goal, anywhere in the world, and that the English language was an essential means of achieving this end. (Similar opinions were of course being expressed by other cultures too, notably the French.)

The strength of feeling on this point has to be appreciated, for it helps to explain the intensity with which the language came to be introduced in many countries, during the period of Empire, and the resources which were poured into it to guarantee the success of its new role. Here is William Russel, writing in 1801:[12]

if many schools were established in different parts of Asia and Africa to instruct the natives, free of all expense, with various premiums [prizes] of British manufacture to the most meritorious pupils, this would be the best preparatory step that Englishmen could adopt for the general admission of their commerce, their opinions, their religion. This would tend

---

[10] As this phrase, also used elsewhere in the book (pp. 10, 120), apparently has a jingoistic ring to some people, it is perhaps necessary to draw attention to its ironic tone. In using it, I intended to suggest, with a Welsh tongue in cheek, that English has been fortunate indeed to do so well – just as someone turning up at a bar 'at the right time' might end up being given a free drink from the person buying a round. This brief excursus into usage would not be necessary if the phrase had not been cited (by Phillipson 1998/1999) as evidence of the supposed triumphalism of the first edition.

[11] Pitman (1873 : 290).   [12] Russel (1801: 93).

to conquer the heart and its affections; which is a far more effectual conquest than that obtained by swords and cannons: and a thousand pounds
expended for tutors, books, and premiums would do more to subdue a
nation of savages than forty thousand expended for artillerymen, bullets,
and gunpowder.

The triumphalist attitude is unpalatable today, but it well illustrates the mood of the time. William White is even more explicit
about the role the English language can play, when it is introduced into a new part of the world. Talking in 1872 about the
many languages of India, he comments:[13]

As we link Calcutta with Bombay, and Bombay with Madras, and by
roads, railways, and telegraphs interlace province with province, we may
in process of time fuse India into unity, and the use and prevalence of
our language may be the register of the progress of that unity.

The register of the progress of that unity. That is the vision which is
repeatedly encountered as we trace the path of English around the
British Empire: the language as a guarantor, as well as a symbol, of
political unity. It is a vision, moreover, which continued to prove
compelling a century later, when the evidence of that Empire was
rapidly vanishing from the atlas. Many of the newly independent
multilingual countries, especially in Africa, chose English as their
official language to enable speakers of their indigenous communities to continue communicating with each other at a national level.
And the concept of language as a political symbol still emerges
every time people perceive the unity of their country to be threatened by minority movements – as we shall see in chapter 5, in
relation to English in present-day USA.

In the context of colonialism, the desire for national linguistic
unity is the other side of the coin from the desire for international
linguistic unity. The language of a colonial power introduces a
new, unifying medium of communication within a colony, but at
the same time it reflects the bonds between that colony and the
home country. In the case of English, these bonds were of especial significance, because of the special nature of the historical

[13] White (1872: 3).

period during which they were being formed. They brought immediate access to a culture which more than any other had been responsible for the Industrial Revolution.

Access to knowledge

As we saw in chapter 1, by the beginning of the nineteenth century, Britain had become the world's leading industrial and trading nation. Its population of 5 million in 1700 more than doubled by 1800, and during that century no country could equal its economic growth, with a gross national product rising, on average, at 2 per cent a year.[14] Most of the innovations of the Industrial Revolution were of British origin: the harnessing of coal, water and steam to drive heavy machinery; the development of new materials, techniques and equipment in a wide range of manufacturing industries; and the emergence of new means of transportation. By 1800, the chief growth areas, in textiles and mining, were producing a range of manufactured goods for export which led to Britain being called the 'workshop of the world'. Names such as Thomas Newcomen, James Watt, Matthew Boulton, Richard Trevithick, George Stephenson, Charles Wheatstone, Michael Faraday, Humphry Davy, Thomas Telford and Henry Bessemer reflect the British achievement of that time.

The linguistic consequences of this achievement were far-reaching. The new terminology of technological and scientific advance had an immediate impact on the language, adding tens of thousands of words to the English lexicon. But, more important, the fact that these innovations were pouring out of an English-speaking country meant that those from abroad who wished to learn about them would need to learn English – and learn it well – if they wished to benefit. Especially after the French Wars (1792–1815), missions of inquiry arrived in Britain from several continental countries, foreign workers were seconded to British factories, and many Britons came to earn a good living abroad, teaching the new methods of industrial production.

[14] Parker (1986: 391).

The magnet of opportunity in Britain attracted several inventors from the Continent, who subsequently became leaders in their field. Here are three famous instances, from the beginning, the middle, and the end of the nineteenth century. The civil engineer Marc Isambard Brunel was born in France, but fled the Revolution to the USA, before moving to England in 1799. William Siemens, the steel manufacturer, was born in Prussia, but settled in London in the 1840s. And Guglielmo Marconi was born in Italy (though his mother was Irish), but received little encouragement there for his experiments, and from 1896 worked in London, where he filed his first patent.

It was not long before similar developments were taking place in America which, by the end of the century, had overtaken Britain as the world's fastest growing economy. There is a corresponding litany of US inventors who maintained the momentum of the Industrial Revolution in Europe and began to rival their European counterparts in fame, as such names as Benjamin Franklin, Thomas Edison, Samuel Morse and Robert Fulton suggest. Gradually, America in turn acted as a magnet for European scholars, such as glaciologist Jean-Louis Agassiz (in 1846), electrical engineer Nikola Tesla (in 1884), and industrial chemist Leo Baekeland (in 1889). When the American research is added to the British, it is possible to suggest that about half of the influential scientific and technological output in the period between 1750 to 1900 would have been written in English. If we analyse the entries in the *Chambers concise dictionary of scientists* (a book which has been praised for its attention to internationalism), we find that 45 per cent of the people from this period were working routinely in an English-language environment, and several more were collaborating with English-speaking scholars.[15]

The nature of the Industrial Revolution would have been very different if it had not been supported by developments which made the new knowledge widely available. Indeed, some of the technology was itself critical in helping the dissemination of ideas. In particular, steam technology revolutionized printing, enabling

[15] Millar, *et al.* (1989).

81

the introduction of the high-speed rotary press and the Linotype machine for casting and setting type, and generating an unprecedented mass of publications in English – technical manuals and leaflets, books of instructions, specialized and popular periodicals, advertisements, and proceedings of learned societies. And as the innovations made their impact on America, the amount of expository material in the English language increased dramatically.

Access to the new knowledge was also much helped by progress in transportation. During the first half of the nineteenth century, the growth of new transport systems, especially the steamship and the railway, began the process of bringing people closer together. During the second half, the growth of new communication systems, especially the telegraph and telephone, made contact between people virtually instantaneous. In 1815, it took four days for news of the Battle of Waterloo to reach London. In 1915, news from the Gallipoli campaign in the Dardanelles was arriving by the hour.

Increasingly rapid and robust methods of transportation transformed the availability of the products of the Industrial Revolution. New methods of mass production demanded new means of mass transportation. In particular, as far as the language was concerned, the distribution of daily newspapers on a large scale would not have been possible without a railway system and, later, a road network capable of carrying increasingly heavy vehicles. Another major step was the arrival of new sources of energy. Edwin L. Drake bored the first oil well in Pennsylvania in 1859, and by 1880 the Standard Oil Company, under John D. Rockefeller and his associates, was controlling the refining of over 90 per cent of all oil produced in the USA.

Standard Oil was but one of several giant organizations to emerge in the USA during the later decades of the century, nurtured by the huge natural resources of the country and the demands of its rapidly growing population. Another was the newspaper empire of William Randolph Hearst. A third was the manufacturing, banking, and transportation empire of financier John Pierpont Morgan. By the turn of the century his banking house had become one of the world's most powerful financial institutions, helping to finance the supply and credit needs of the Allies in the First World War, and much of the cost of post-war European reconstruction. The only country to have developed comparable financial and industrial strengths, during the last quarter of the nineteenth century, was Germany; but these were to disappear following defeat in 1918, leaving the ground clear for American economic domination.

The early nineteenth century had seen the rapid growth of the international banking system, especially in Germany, Britain, and the USA. The new organizations supported the fortunes of the developing industrial companies, handled government securities, and facilitated the growth of world trade and investment. In particular, the less wealthy countries of Europe, as well as the new colonies further afield, urgently needed to attract foreign investment. Firms such as Rothschilds and Morgans grew in response to these needs, and London and New York became the investment capitals of the world.

In 1914, Britain and the USA were together investing over £4,500 thousand million abroad – three times as much as France and almost four times as much as Germany. The resulting 'economic imperialism', as it was later called, brought a fresh dimension to the balance of linguistic power. 'Access to knowledge' now became 'access to knowledge about how to get financial backing'. If the metaphor 'money talks' has any meaning at all, those were the days when it was shouting loudly – and the language in which it was shouting was chiefly English.

Taken for granted

The story of English throughout this period is one of rapid expansion and diversification, with innovation after innovation coming to use the language as a primary or sole means of expression. It is not possible to identify cause and effect. So many developments were taking place at the same time that we can only point to the emergence, by the end of the nineteenth century, of a climate of largely unspoken opinion which had made English the natural choice for progress. We shall see this climate present in all of the domains reviewed in chapter 4.

'Unspoken' is an important word. Insofar as it is possible to find out about the decision-making processes which were taking place at the time, there is hardly any conscious justification for the role of English. When the first radio stations were coming on air (p. 95), no one seems to have spent any time debating whether or not they should broadcast in English. There was plenty of discussion about what **kind** of English should be used, of course; but the choice of English in the first place was simply not an issue. Nor was it an issue for the other developments which were catching the public eye as the new century dawned.

There was nothing novel about taking English for granted in this way. Given the colonial origins of English in the countries of the inner circle (p. 60), the standing of the language could never have been in doubt. There was no competition from other languages, no crisis of linguistic identity on the part of the colonial power, and thus no threat. No argument for making English official is found in any of the documents which are significant for the history of Britain, and English has never been formally declared the official language of that country. Nor was English singled out for mention when the Constitution of the United States was being written. Rulings are needed to regulate conflict. None of the conflicts which arose were capable of threatening the status of English; consequently, there was no need for rulings.

However, as the twentieth century progressed, situations arose where repeatedly the status of English (and other ex-colonial languages) was called into question. The typical scenario was one where speakers of a language felt their language needed protection because its existence was being threatened by a more dominant language. In such cases, the dominant power would sometimes take measures to preserve it (usually, after forceful pressure from the members of the minority community) by giving it special recognition. This has happened occasionally, and especially in recent decades, among the countries of the inner circle: for example, some degree of official status has now been given to Welsh in Wales, Irish Gaelic in Ireland, French in Quebec, and Maori in New Zealand. And in each case, it has proved necessary to pay attention to the corresponding official role of English, in these territories, also as a protective measure. Here, the issue is one of identity.

Among the countries of the outer circle, where English is used as a second language, the decision to give English official status has usually been made in order to avoid the problem of having to choose between competing local languages. English is perceived to be a 'neutral' language, in this respect. Examples where this has happened include Ghana and Nigeria. Not everyone believes English to be neutral, of course, as we shall see in chapter 5, in relation to such cases as Kenya. But the decision, when it is made, is based on political expediency.

In a country where 95 per cent or so of the population speak English, as in Britain and the USA, it might be thought that a problem could not arise. But even small changes in the social balance of a population can have serious linguistic consequences. When large social changes take place, such as have happened through immigration during the past century, the potential effects on language policy and planning can be far-reaching, as we shall see later in relation to the current debate over the role of English in the USA.

But, in 1900, there was no prospect of any such debate. English had become the dominant language of global politics and economy, and all the signs were that it would remain so. Its status was not in question, and the role of the USA in its future was clear. A notable observation was that of Bismarck, who in 1898 was asked by a journalist what he considered to be the decisive factor in modern history; he replied, 'The fact that the North Americans speak English'.[16] To maintain the standing of the language, all that was needed was a period of consolidation and expansion, and this, as the next chapter amply demonstrates, was soon forthcoming.

[16] Reported in Nunberg (2000).

4
Why English? The cultural legacy

The first steps in the political consolidation of English were taken during the decision-making which followed the First World War, in 1919. The mandates system introduced by the League of Nations transferred former German colonies in Africa, the Middle East, Asia, and the Pacific to the supervision of the victors, and English language influence grew immensely in the areas which came to be mediated directly by Britain (such as in Palestine, Cameroon and Tanganyika) or by other English-speaking nations: examples include Australia (in Papua New Guinea), New Zealand (in Samoa) and South Africa (in South-West Africa – present-day Namibia).

But the growth of linguistic influence through political expansion was already on the wane. Far more important for the English language, in the post-war world, was the way in which the cultural legacies of the colonial era and the technological revolution were being felt on an international scale. English was now emerging as a medium of communication in growth areas which would gradually shape the character of twentieth-century domestic and professional life.

International relations

The League of Nations was the first of many modern international alliances to allocate a special place to English in its proceedings:

English was one of the two official languages (the other was French), and all documents were printed in both. The League was created as part of the Treaty of Versailles in 1920, and at the time of its First Assembly, it had forty-two members, several from outside Europe. The importance of a lingua franca, with such an extended membership, was obvious. The League was replaced in 1945 by the United Nations, where the role of the lingua franca became even more critical. The UN now consists of over fifty distinct organs, programmes, and specialized agencies, as well as many regional and functional commissions, standing committees, expert bodies, and other organizations. English is one of the official languages within all of these structures.

The language plays an official or working role in the proceedings of most other major international political gatherings, in all parts of the world. Examples include the Association of South-East Asian Nations, the Commonwealth, the Council of Europe, the European Union and the North Atlantic Treaty Organization. English is the only official language of the Organization of Petroleum Exporting Countries, for example, and the only working language of the European Free Trade Association. Unless a body has a highly restricted membership (such as one consisting only of Arabic-speaking states or only of Spanish-speaking states), the choice of a lingua franca has to be made, and English is the first choice of most. However, even the restricted-membership meetings recognize the value of English: although their proceedings may not be expressed in English, the reports they issue for the wider public at the end of their meeting, and the statements which their officials make to the world media, usually are.

The extent to which English is used in this way is often not appreciated. In 1995–6, there were about 12,500 international organizations in the world.[1] About a third list the languages they use in an official or working capacity. A sample of 500 of these (taken from the beginning of the alphabet) showed that 85 per cent (424) made official use of English – far more than any other language. French was the only other language to show up strongly, with 49 per cent (245) using it officially. Thirty other languages

---

[1] Union of International Associations (1996).

also attracted occasional official status, but only Arabic, Spanish, and German achieved over 10 per cent recognition.

Of particular significance is the number of organizations in this sample which use **only** English to carry on their affairs: 169 – a third. This reliance is especially noticeable in Asia and the Pacific, where about 90 per cent of international bodies carry on their proceedings entirely in English. Many scientific organizations (such as the African Association of Science Editors, the Cairo Demographic Centre and Baltic Marine Biologists) are also English-only. By contrast, only a small number of international bodies (13 per cent) make no official use of English at all: most of these are French organizations, dealing chiefly with francophone concerns.

The reliance on English is by no means restricted to science, however. Several international sporting organizations work only in English, such as the African Hockey Federation, the Asian Amateur Athletic Association and the Association of Oceania National Olympic Committees; and when these organizations hold international competitions, the language automatically becomes the lingua franca of the gathering. English is used as the sole official language in relation to a wide range of topics, as is illustrated by the All-African People's Organization, Architects Regional Council Asia and the Asian Buddhist Conference for Peace.

These trends are reflected even in Europe, where we might expect other languages to be playing a more dominant role. We can see this if we examine the *Yearbook* organizations whose names begin with *Euro-*. Out of a sample of 1,000 of these, 440 specified the official or working languages they used. Almost all used English as an official language – 435, a remarkable 99 per cent. French was used by 63 per cent (278) and German by 40 per cent (176). English + French + German was the most popular European combination.

In Europe, too, organizations which work only in English are surprisingly common, especially in science. The European Academy of Anaesthesiology and the European Academy of Facial Surgery use only English in their proceedings, as do the European Association of Cancer Research and the European Association of Fish Pathology. Bodies from other domains include the

European Air Law Association, the European Bridge League and the European Aluminium Association. One of the few organizations which makes no official use of English at all is the European Federation of Perfumery Retailers.

Several bodies use English in more than one way. For example, the Afro-Asian Rural Reconstruction Organization has three official languages – English, Arabic and French – but for its working language it uses only English. Europage, which unites the yellow-pages publishers of the European Union, lists Dutch, English, French, German, Italian and Spanish as official languages, but adds that only English is to be used for correspondence.

The overriding impression is that, wherever in the world an organization is based, English is the chief auxiliary language. The Andean Commission of Jurists recognizes Spanish – and English. The German anatomical association Anatomische Gesellschaft recognizes German – and English. The Arab Air Carriers Association recognizes Arabic – and English.

A different kind of role for English is encountered at meetings where a large number of nations each has the right to participate using its own language. The European Union is the most complex example, where already by 1996 the fifteen member states were presenting a situation in which over a hundred pairs of languages required translation and interpreting services (French/English, French/German, French/Finnish, etc.). It is impossible to find expert translators and interpreters for all language pairs, or to provide maximum coverage on all occasions, so efforts have been made to find alternative procedures (other than asking some of the countries to give up their official status). The situation has become increasingly serious as more members join the Union, and will eventually require a radical overhaul (a further 12 applications were pending in 2002).

Several solutions to this problem have been proposed, such as the use of a 'relay' system. If there is no Finnish/Greek translator available, for instance, English might be used as an intermediary language – or 'interlingua', as it is sometimes called. One person would translate a speech from Finnish into English; another would translate the result from English into Greek. Any language could be so used, but English is the one which seems to be most often employed in this way. In 1995, 42 per cent of European Union citizens claimed to be able to converse in English – well ahead of German (31 per cent) and French (29 per cent). This figure had risen to 47 per cent by 2002.[2]

International politics operates at several levels and in many different ways, but the presence of English is usually not far away. A political protest may surface in the form of an official question to a government minister, a peaceful lobby outside an embassy, a street riot, or a bomb. When the television cameras present the event to a world audience, it is notable how often a message in English can be seen on a banner or placard as part of the occasion. Whatever the mother tongue of the protesters, they know that their cause will gain maximum impact if it is expressed through the medium of English. A famous instance of this occurred a few years ago in India, where a march supporting Hindi and opposing English was seen on world television: most of the banners were in Hindi, but one astute marcher carried a prominent sign which read 'Death to English' – thereby enabling the voice of his group to reach much further around the world than would otherwise have been possible.

The media

These days, any consideration of politics leads inevitably to a consideration of the role of the media. Indeed, if the erstwhile anonymous author of the novel *Primary colors* is to be believed, successful access to the media is the guarantor of political achievement, and much of a campaign staff member's time is devoted to ensuring that this will happen. At one point, Henry Burton, the governor's aide, reflects ruefully on the way the election campaign was going wrong:[3]

The Sunday morning papers had Freddie Picker being endorsed by the governor of Pennsylvania and most of the state's congressional delegation. I read it as a civilian might, without a twinge. There had been days,

[2] European Commission (2002b). See also Baker and Prys Jones (1998: 259).
[3] Anonymous (1996: 330).

90

months, when I could soar or dive on the hint of a nuance in a one-paragraph item buried in *The Washington Post*; that had been my life. But the campaign was over for me now.

In the novel, the media are at the centre of everyone's life – the press, radio, advertising, and especially television. Even the 'hint of a nuance' can make a difference.

- *The press*

The English language has been an important medium of the press for nearly 400 years. As early as the first decades of the seventeenth century, several European countries were publishing rudimentary newspapers, but censorship, taxation, wars, and other constraints allowed little growth.[4] Progress was much greater in Britain, though even in that country periods of censorship greatly limited newspaper content until towards the end of the century. The *Weekley Newes* began to appear (irregularly) from 1622; the *London Gazette* in 1666; and *Lloyd's News* in 1696, providing general news as well as information about shipping. American developments, beginning somewhat later, included the *Boston News-Letter* (1704), *The New-York Gazette* (1725), and the New York City *Daily Advertiser* (1785). The beginning of the eighteenth century in Britain saw the rise and fall of *The Tatler* (1709) and *The Spectator* (1711), while the end brought the arrival of *The Times* (1788) and *The Observer* (1791).

The nineteenth century was the period of greatest progress, thanks to the introduction of new printing technology and new methods of mass production and transportation. It also saw the development of a truly independent press, chiefly fostered in the USA, where there were some 400 daily newspapers by 1850, and nearly 2,000 by the turn of the century. Censorship and other restrictions continued in Continental Europe during the early decades, however, which meant that the provision of popular news in languages other than English developed much more slowly.

---

[4] For the history of the press, see *Encyclopaedia Britannica* (1986, Vol. XXVI: 483ff.).

Massive circulations were achieved by such papers as the *New York Herald* (1833) and *New York Tribune* (1841). Sensationalism brought even larger sales, and newspaper empires grew. In Britain, taxation restricted the growth of the press in the first half of the century, but *The Times* continued to grow in stature throughout the period, and the abolition of the Stamp Tax in 1855 prompted a flood of publications. By the end of the century, popular journalism, in the form of *The Daily Mail* (1896), brought Britain into line with America. From then on, no headlines screamed with greater visual force from the news-stands of the world than those published in the English language.

The high profile given to English in the popular press was reinforced by the way techniques of news gathering developed. The mid nineteenth century saw the growth of the major news agencies, especially following the invention of the telegraph (they were long known as 'wire services'). Paul Julius Reuter started an office in Aachen, but soon moved to London, where in 1851 he launched the agency which now bears his name. By 1870 Reuters had acquired more territorial news monopolies than any of its Continental competitors. With the emergence in 1856 of the New York Associated Press (which later developed into the Associated Press), the majority of the information being transmitted along the telegraph wires of the world was in English.

Newspapers are not solely international media: they play an important role in the identity of a local community. Most papers are for home circulation, and are published in a home language. It is therefore impossible to gain an impression of the power of English from the bare statistics of newspaper production and circulation. None the less, according to the data compiled by the *Encyclopaedia Britannica* in 2002 about 57 per cent of the world's newspapers were being published in those countries (see the list at the end of chapter 2) where the English language has special status, and it is reasonable to assume that the majority of these would be in English.[5]

More important – though much more subjective – are estimates of the influence of individual newspapers on a world scale.

[5] *Encyclopaedia Britannica* (2002: 850ff.).

In one such table,[6] the top five papers were all in English: top was *The New York Times*, followed by *The Washington Post*, *The Wall Street Journal*, and the two British papers *The Times* and *The Sunday Times*. Of particular importance are those English-language newspapers intended for a global readership, such as the *International Herald-Tribune, US Weekly* and *International Guardian*.

A similar story could be told in relation to the publication of periodicals, magazines, pamphlets, digests and other ephemera. Information is much more sparse (only half the countries in the world have provided data for comparative listings), but it would seem that about a quarter of the world's periodicals are published in English-status countries. This total refers to all kinds of publication, of course – literary reviews, hobby journals, comics, fanzines (fan group magazines), pornographic literature, technical reviews, scholarly journals and much more.

When the focus is restricted to individual genres, the figures vary dramatically. As a visit to any university library shows, in any country, most academic journals with an international readership are published in English. In the 1990s the journal *Linguistics Abstracts* was reviewing the content of over 160 linguistics journals worldwide: nearly 70 per cent were published entirely in English. In the physical sciences, the figure may reach 80 per cent or more. By contrast, material aimed at younger people, such as comics and fanzines, is often in a local language.

- *Advertising*

Towards the end of the nineteenth century, a combination of social and economic factors led to a dramatic increase in the use of advertisements in publications, especially in the more industrialized countries.[7] Mass production had increased the flow of goods and was fostering competition; consumer purchasing power was growing; and new printing techniques were providing fresh display possibilities. In the USA, publishers realized that income from advertising would allow them to lower the selling price of

---

[6] Wallechinsky, Wallace and Wallace (1977: 114).
[7] For the early history of advertising, see Presbrey (1929), Elliott (1962).

their magazines, and thus hugely increase circulation. In 1893 *McClure's Magazine, Cosmopolitan* and *Munsey's Magazine* all adopted this tactic, and within a few years, the 'ten-cent magazine' had trebled its sales. Before long, publications in which over half of the pages were given over to advertising became the norm, from the turn of the century increasingly in colour, leading eventually to the arrival of the wide range of glossy magazines and newspaper supplements available today. Two-thirds of a modern newspaper, especially in the USA, may be devoted to advertising.

English in advertising began very early on, when the weekly newspapers began to carry items about books, medicines, tea, and other domestic products. An advertising supplement appeared in the *London Gazette* in 1666, and within a century advertisements had grown both in number and in style – so much so that Dr Johnson was led to comment caustically about their 'magnificence of promise and... eloquence sometimes sublime and sometimes pathetic'.[8] During the nineteenth century the advertising slogan became a feature of the medium, as did the famous 'trade name'. 'It pays to advertise' itself became a US slogan in the 1920s. Many products which are now household names received a special boost in that decade, such as Ford, Coca Cola, Kodak and Kellogg.

The media capitalized on the brevity with which a product could be conveyed to an audience – even if the people were passing at speed in one of the new methods of transportation. Posters, billboards, electric displays, shop signs and other techniques became part of the everyday scene. As international markets grew, the 'outdoor media' began to travel the world, and their prominence in virtually every town and city is now one of the most noticeable global manifestations of English language use. The English advertisements are not always more numerous, in countries where English has no special status, but they are usually the most noticeable.

In all of this, it is the English of American products which rules. During the 1950s, the proportion of gross national income devoted to advertising was much higher in the USA than anywhere

[8] In *The Idler* (1758).

else: in 1953, for example, it was 2.6 per cent, compared with 1.5 per cent in Britain. Nearly $6,000 million were devoted to advertising in the USA in 1950, and this rapidly increased as advertisers began to see the potential of television. Other languages began to feel the effects: in Italian, for example, a single verb sums up the era: *cocacolonizzare*, based on *coca cola* and *colonize*. *Macdonaldization* is a more recent example.

The impact was less marked in Europe, where TV advertising was more strictly controlled, but once commercial channels developed, there was a rapid period of catching up, in which American experience and influence were pervasive. The advertising agencies came into their own. By 1972, only three of the world's top thirty agencies were not US-owned (two in Japan and one in Britain). The official language of international advertising bodies, such as the European Association of Advertising Agencies, is invariably English.

- *Broadcasting*

It took many decades of experimental research in physics, chiefly in Britain and America, before it was possible to send the first radio telecommunication signals through the air, without wires (hence the name 'wireless telegraphy').[9] Marconi's system, built in 1895, carried telegraph code signals over a distance of one mile. Six years later, his signals had crossed the Atlantic Ocean; by 1918, they had reached Australia. English was the first language to be transmitted by radio, when US physicist Reginald A. Fessenden broadcast music, poetry, and a short talk to Atlantic shipping from Brant Rock, Massachusetts, USA, on Christmas Eve 1906.

Within twenty-five years of Marconi's first transmission, public broadcasting became a reality. The first commercial radio station was KDKA in Pittsburgh, Pennsylvania, which broadcast its first programme in November 1920 – an account of the Harding–Cox presidential election results. By 1922, in the USA, over 500 broadcasting stations had been licensed; and by 1995, the total was around 5,000 (each for AM and for FM commercial stations).

---

[9] For the history of broadcasting, see Crisell (2002).

Advertising revenue eventually became the chief means of support, as it later did for television.

In Britain, experimental broadcasts were being made as early as 1919, and the British Broadcasting Company (later, Corporation) was established in 1922. It was a monopoly: no other broadcasting company was allowed until the creation of the Independent Television Authority in 1954. In contrast with the USA, BBC revenue came not from advertising, but from royalties on broadcasting equipment and a public licence system (eventually the only revenue). The first director-general of the BBC, John Reith, developed a concept of public-service broadcasting – to inform, educate, and entertain – which proved to be highly influential abroad.

During the early 1920s, English-language broadcasting began in Canada, Australia and New Zealand. The Indian Broadcasting Company had stations in Bombay and Calcutta by 1927. Most European countries commenced radio services during the same period. As services proliferated, the need for international agreements (for example, over the use of wavelengths) became urgent. Several organizations now exist, the largest being the International Telecommunications Union, created as early as 1865 to handle the problems of telegraphy.

There are also several important regional organizations, such as the Commonwealth Broadcasting Association and the European Broadcasting Union, as well as cultural and educational organizations, such as the London-based International Broadcast Institute. In these cases, we find a growing reliance on English as a lingua franca, corresponding to that found in the world of international politics. The Asia–Pacific Broadcasting Union, for example, uses only English as an official language.

A similar dramatic expansion later affected public television. The world's first high-definition service, provided by the BBC, began in London in 1936. In the USA, the National Broadcasting Company was able to provide a regular service in 1939. Within a year there were over twenty TV stations operating in the USA, and although the constraints imposed by the Second World War brought a setback, by 1995 the total number of stations had grown to over 1500. Ten million TV receivers were in use by 1951; by 1990 the figure was approaching 200 million. There was a proportional growth in Britain, which had issued over 300,000 TV licences by 1950. Other countries were much slower to enter the television age, and none has ever achieved the levels of outreach found in the USA, where a 2002 survey reported almost one receiver per person,[10] and where each person spent almost 1,000 hours watching TV during the year.

We can only speculate about how these media developments must have influenced the growth of world English. A casual pass through the wavelengths of a radio receiver shows that no one language rules the airwaves, and there are no statistics on the proportion of time devoted to English-language programmes the world over, or on how much time is spent listening to such programmes. Only a few indirect indications exist: for example, in 1994 about 45 per cent of the world's radio receivers were in those countries where the English language has a special status; but what such figures say in real terms about exposure to English is anyone's guess.

A more specific indication is broadcasting aimed specifically at audiences in other countries. Such programmes were introduced in the 1920s, but Britain did not develop its services until the next decade. The international standing of BBC programmes, especially its news broadcasts, achieved a high point during the Second World War, when they helped to raise morale in German-occupied territories. The World Service of the BBC, launched (as the Empire Service) in 1932, though much cut back in recent years, in 2001 was still broadcasting over 1,000 hours per week to a worldwide audience of 153 million and reaching 120 capital cities, with a listening audience in English estimated at 42 million.[11] BBC English Radio produces over 100 hours of bilingual and all-English programmes weekly. London Radio Services, a publicly funded radio syndicator, offers a daily international news service to over 10,000 radio stations worldwide, chiefly in English.

Although later to develop, the USA rapidly overtook Britain, becoming the leading provider of English-language services

[10] *Encyclopaedia Britannica* (2002: 850ff.).   [11] Byford (2001).

abroad. The Voice of America, the external broadcasting service of the US Information Agency, was not founded until 1942, but it came into its own during the Cold War years. By the 1980s, it was broadcasting from the USA worldwide in English and forty-five other languages. Along with the foreign-based Radio Liberty and Radio Free Europe, the US output amounted to nearly 2,000 hours a week – not far short of the Soviet Union's total. Other sources include the American Forces Radio and Television Service, which broadcasts through a network of local stations all over the world. The International Broadcast Station offers a shortwave service to Latin America in English and certain other languages. Radio New York World Wide provides an English-language service to Europe, Africa and the Caribbean. And channels with a religious orientation also often broadcast widely in English: for example, World International Broadcasters transmits to Europe, the Middle East, and North Africa.

Most other countries showed sharp increases in external broadcasting during the post-War years, and several launched English-language radio programmes, such as the Soviet Union, Italy, Japan, Luxembourg, The Netherlands, Germany and Sweden. No comparative data are available about how many people listen to each of the languages provided by these services. However, if we list the languages in which these countries broadcast, it is noticeable that only one of these languages has a place on each of the lists: English.

- *Cinema*

The new technologies which followed the discovery of electrical power fundamentally altered the nature of home and public entertainment, and provided fresh directions for the development of the English language. Broadcasting was obviously one of these, but that medium was never – according to the influential views of Lord Reith – to be identified solely with the provision of entertainment. This observation did not apply in the case of the motion picture industry.

The technology of this industry has many roots in Europe and America during the nineteenth century, with Britain and

France providing an initial impetus to the artistic and commercial development of the cinema from 1895. However, the years preceding and during the First World War stunted the growth of a European film industry, and dominance soon passed to America, which oversaw from 1915 the emergence of the feature film, the star system, the movie mogul, and the grand studio, all based in Hollywood, California.[12]

As a result, when sound was added to the technology in the late 1920s, it was the English language which suddenly came to dominate the movie world. It is difficult to find accurate data, but several publications of the period provide clues. For example, in 1933 appeared the first edition of *The picturegoer's who's who and encyclopaedia of the screen today*.[13] Of the 44 studios listed, 32 were American or British (the others were German and French). Of the 2,466 artistes listed, only 85 (3 per cent) were making movies in languages other than English. Of the 340 directors, 318 (94 per cent) were involved only in English-language works. As an English-language reference book, there is bound to be some bias in the coverage – few movie stars are listed from non-European countries, for example – but the overall impression is probably not far from the truth.

Despite the growth of the film industry in other countries in later decades, English-language movies still dominate the medium, with Hollywood coming to rely increasingly on a small number of annual productions aimed at huge audiences – such as *Star Wars*, *Titanic* and *The Lord of the Rings*. It is unusual to find a blockbuster movie produced in a language other than English. In 2002, according to the listings in the *BFI film and television handbook*, over 80 per cent of all feature films given a theatrical release were in English.[14] The Oscar system has always been English-language oriented (though the category of best foreign film was recognized in 1947), but there is a strong English-language presence in most other film festivals too. Half of the Best Film awards ever given at the Cannes Film Festival, for example, have been to English-language productions.

---

[12] For the history of cinema, see Nowell-Smith (1996).
[13] Picturegoer Weekly (1933).   [14] Dyja (2001).

By the mid-1990s, according to film critic David Robinson in an *Encyclopaedia Britannica* review,[15] the USA controlled about 85 per cent of the world film market, with Hollywood films dominating the box offices in most countries. A cinema in Denmark would very likely be showing the same range of films as one in Spain, and most would be English-language films (usually subtitled). A notable development was to see this dominance manifest itself even in countries where there has been a strong national tradition of film-making, such as Japan, France, Italy and Germany. Before 1990, France was continuing to attract majority audiences for its own films (the only European country to do so); in recent years, French-language films may account for as little as 30 per cent of the national box office.

The influence of movies on the viewing audience is uncertain, but many observers agree with the view of the German director Wim Wenders: 'People increasingly believe in what they see and they buy what they believe in ... People use, drive, wear, eat and buy what they see in the movies.'[16] If this is so, then the fact that most movies are made in the English language must surely be significant, at least in the long term.

- *Popular music*

The cinema was one of two new entertainment technologies which emerged at the end of the nineteenth century: the other was the recording industry.[17] Here too the English language was early in evidence. When in 1877 Thomas A. Edison devised the phonograph, the first machine that could both record and reproduce sound, the first words to be recorded were 'What God hath wrought', followed by the words of the nursery-rhyme 'Mary had a little lamb'.

Most of the subsequent technical developments took place in the USA. Gramophone records soon came to replace cylinders. The first US patent for magnetic tape was as early as 1927. Columbia Records introduced the long-playing (LP) disk in 1948.

---

[15] Robinson (1995: 245).   [16] Reported ibid.
[17] For the history of sound recording, see Gronow, Saunio and Moseley (1998).

All the major recording companies in popular music had English-language origins. The oldest active record label is the US firm Columbia (from 1898); others are HMV (originally British), merged in 1931 with Columbia to form EMI. Other labels include Brunswick, established in the USA in 1916, and Decca, established in Britain in 1929.

Radio sets around the world hourly testify to the dominance of English in the popular music scene today. Many people make their first contact with English in this way. It is a dominance which is a specifically twentieth-century phenomenon, but the role of English in this genre starts much earlier. During the nineteenth century, popular music was embedded within the dance halls, beer halls, and popular theatres of innumerable European cities, producing thousands of songs whose content ranged from the wildly comic and satirical to the desperately sentimental. The British music hall was a major influence on popular trends – much more so, it is thought, than the French and German cabarets and operettas of the period.

Travelling British entertainers visited the USA, which developed its own music hall traditions in the form of vaudeville. Touring minstrel groups became popular from the middle of the nineteenth century. Songwriters such as Stephen Foster found their compositions (over 200 hits, including 'Old Folks at Home', 'Camptown Races', and 'Beautiful Dreamer') circulating on an unprecedented scale through the rapidly growing network of theatres. By the turn of the century, Tin Pan Alley (the popular name for the Broadway-centred song-publishing industry) was a reality, and was soon known worldwide as the chief source of US popular music.

A similar trend can be seen in relation to the more 'up-market' genres. During the early twentieth century, European light opera (typified by Strauss and Offenbach) developed an English-language dimension. Several major composers were immigrants to the USA, such as the Czech-born Rudolf Friml (who arrived in 1906) and Hungarian-born Sigmund Romberg (who arrived in 1909), or they were the children of immigrants (such as George Gershwin). The 1920s proved to be a remarkable decade for the operetta, as a result, with such famous examples as Romberg's *The Student Prince* (1924) and Friml's *Rose Marie*. The same decade also saw the rapid growth of the musical, a distinctively US product, and the rise to fame of such composers as Jerome Kern and George Gershwin, and later Cole Porter and Richard Rodgers.

The rapidly growing broadcasting companies were greedy for fresh material, and thousands of new works each year found an international audience in ways that could not have been conceived of a decade before. The availability of mass-produced gramophone records allowed the works of these composers ('songs from the shows') to travel the world in physical form. Soon the words of the hit songs were being learned by heart and reproduced with varying accents in cabarets and music halls all over Europe – as well as in the homes of the well-to-do.

Jazz, too, influenced so much by the folk blues of black plantation workers, had its linguistic dimension. Blues singers such as Ma Rainey and Bessie Smith were part of the US music-hall scene from the early years of the twentieth century. Other genres emerged – hillbilly songs, country music, gospel songs, and a wide range of folk singing. The vocal element in the dance music of such swing bands as Glenn Miller's swept the world in the 1930s and 1940s. And, in due course, the words and beat of rhythm and blues grew into rock and roll.

When modern popular music arrived, it was almost entirely an English scene. The pop groups of two chief English-speaking nations were soon to dominate the recording world: Bill Haley and the Comets and Elvis Presley in the USA; the Beatles and the Rolling Stones in the UK. Mass audiences for pop singers became a routine feature of the world scene from the 1960s. No other single source has spread the English language around the youth of the world so rapidly and so pervasively. In 1996, Nick Reynolds, a popular music producer of the BBC World Service, commented: 'Pop music is virtually the only field in which the British have led the world in the past three decades', and adds, echoing the accolade made some 200 years ago (p. 80), 'Britain is still the pop workshop of the planet'.[18]

---

[18] Reynolds (1996: 9).

In the 2000s, the English-language character of the international pop music world is extraordinary. Although every country has its popular singers, singing in their own language, only a few manage to break through into the international arena, and in order to do so it seems they need to be singing in English. The 1990 edition of *The Penguin encyclopedia of popular music* was an instructive guide to the 1990s decade: of the 557 pop groups it included, 549 (99 per cent) worked entirely or predominantly in English; of the 1,219 solo vocalists, 1,156 (95 per cent) sang in English. The mother tongue of the singers was apparently irrelevant. The entire international career of ABBA, the Swedish group with over twenty hit records in the 1970s, was in English. Most contributions to the annual Eurovision Song Contest are in English −17 titles out of 24 in 2002.

These days, the sound of the English language, through the medium of popular song, is heard wherever there is a radio set. It is a commonplace tourist experience to hear a familiar English refrain in a coffee bar, bus station or elevator, or simply issuing from the window of a house on almost any street in any town. Often, it is a source of despair. We travel to 'get away from it all', and 'it' follows us everywhere we go. We enter a local nightclub in our holiday destination, and all we hear is the current top twenty. 'Happy birthday to you' is widely sung at children's birthday parties in many countries. Finding genuinely local music can be extremely difficult. Several commentators have remarked on the way in which western popular music has threatened the life of ethnic musical traditions everywhere.

At the same time, other commentators have drawn attention to the way popular music in the English language has had a profound and positive impact on the nature of modern popular culture in general. As the lyrics (as distinct from the tunes) of Bob Dylan, Bob Marley, John Lennon, Joan Baez and others spread around the world, during the 1960s and 1970s, English for the younger generation in many countries became a symbol of freedom, rebellion and modernism. The social, political, and spiritual messages carried by the words (such as 'We Shall Overcome') resounded at gatherings in many countries, providing many people with a first – and often highly charged – experience of the unifying power of English in action. And the language has continued to play this role, being the medium of such international projects as 'Live Aid'.

International travel

The reasons for travelling abroad are many and various. They range from routine business trips to annual holidays, and from religious pilgrimages and sports competitions to military interventions. Each journey has immediate linguistic consequences – a language has to be interpreted, learned, imposed – and over time a travelling trend can develop into a major influence. If there is a contemporary movement towards world English use, therefore, we would expect it to be particularly noticeable in this domain. And so it is.

In the tourist industry, for example, worldwide international arrivals approached 700 million in 2000. The leading tourism earner and spender is the USA. In 2001, according to the World Tourism Organization, the USA earned over $72,000 million from tourism – over twice as much as its nearest rival, Spain; it also spent nearly $59,000 million on tourism – ahead of Germany and the UK. The predominance seems set to continue, notwithstanding the initial impact on international travel caused by the terrorist attacks on 11 September 2001 in New York.[19] Money talks very loudly in tourism – if only because the tourist has extra money to spend while on holiday. In the tourist spots of the world, accordingly, the signs in the shop windows are most commonly in English. Restaurant menus tend to have a parallel version in English. Credit card facilities, such as American Express and Mastercard, are most noticeably in English. And among the destitute who haunt the tourist locations, the smattering of foreign language which is used to sell artefacts or to beg money from the passing visitor is usually a pidgin form of English.

[19] Estimated to be only 0.6% down by the World Tourism Organization, reported in its regional series, Tourism Market Trends (September 2002). Other data in this paragraph are derived from this series.

Move away from the regular tourist routes, however, and English soon becomes conspicuous by its absence. It is important not to forget the fact that, even if one third of the world is now regularly exposed to English, as was suggested in chapter 1, this still means that two thirds are not. We need only to walk up a side street in a city, or pause at a village on our way to a destination, to experience the world's remarkable linguistic diversity. The more we know about the language(s) of the country we are exploring, the more we shall be rewarded with a visit that is insightful and comfortable.

By contrast, for those whose international travel brings them into a world of package holidays, business meetings, academic conferences, international conventions, community rallies, sporting occasions, military occupations and other 'official' gatherings, the domains of transportation and accommodation are mediated through the use of English as an auxiliary language. Safety instructions on international flights and sailings, information about emergency procedures in hotels, and directions to major locations are now increasingly in English alongside local languages. Most notices which tell us to fasten our seatbelts, find the lifeboat stations, or check the location of the emergency stairs give us an option in English. In some cities, the trend towards English has been especially noticeable. An English-speaking visitor to Tokyo in 1985 would have found city travel a largely impenetrable experience without an English-language map; but by 1995, English road signs had become commonplace.

The role of the military, in the spread of English, is difficult to evaluate. It is obvious that the language of an invading army, or an army of occupation, must have an immediate effect on a community, but how long this effect lasts is an open question. American songs were exported both in the Boer War and the First World War, and American Forces Network radio, in particular, ensured that English was widely heard in Europe during and after the Second World War. The presence of US and British forces in large numbers would certainly have brought the local inhabitants into contact with English-speaking culture more rapidly than would otherwise have been the case, if only in such areas as advertising and popular music. It is even possible that in some instances the effects would be long-lasting – perhaps as individuals returned to marry or work in a former war zone. This especially happened in Europe after 1945. But there is little evidence to go on.

A similar point could be made about the 1990s, which saw the presence of English-speaking troops on peace-keeping missions in Bosnia, the Middle East, Central Africa and elsewhere and in Afghanistan since 2001. UN officers are routinely heard on TV commenting on the way a crisis is developing, and the language used to the cameras is almost always English. But is it likely that an English-language presence of a few months, or even years, would have a long-term influence on local language awareness? We can only speculate.

International safety

A special aspect of safety is the way that the language has come to be used as a means of controlling international transport operations, especially on water and in the air. As world travel has grown, more people and goods are being transported more quickly and simultaneously to more places than ever before. The communicative demands placed on air and sea personnel, given the variety of language backgrounds involved, have thus grown correspondingly. In such circumstances, the use of a lingua franca has proved of great worth.

English has long been recognized as the international language of the sea, and in recent years there have been attempts to refine its use to make it as efficient as possible. Larger and faster ships pose greater navigational hazards. Shipping routes continually alter and present fresh problems of traffic flow. Radio and satellite systems have greatly extended a ship's communicative range. In such circumstances, mariners need to make their speech clear and unambiguous, to reduce the possibility of confusion in the sending and receiving of messages.

In 1980, a project was set up to produce Essential English for International Maritime Use – often referred to as 'Seaspeak'.[20]

[20] Weeks, Glover, Strevens and Johnson (1984).

The recommendations related mainly to communication by VHF radio, and included procedures for initiating, maintaining, and terminating conversations, as well as a recommended grammar, vocabulary and structure for messages on a wide range of maritime subjects. For example, instead of saying 'What did you say?', 'I didn't hear you', 'Would you please say that once more', and many other possibilities, Seaspeak recommends a single phrase: 'Say again'. Likewise, bearings and courses are given with three-figure values ('009 degrees', not '9 degrees') and dates are signalled using prefixes ('day one-three, month zero-five, year one-nine-nine-six'). Though it is far more restricted than everyday language, Seaspeak has considerable expressive power.

Progress has also been made in recent years in devising systems of unambiguous communication between organizations which are involved in handling emergencies on the ground – notably, the fire service, the ambulance service and the police. When the Channel Tunnel between Britain and France came into operation for the first time in 1994, it presented new possibilities for international confusion. Research has therefore been ongoing into a way of standardizing communication between the UK and the Continent of Europe: it is called 'Police Speak'.[21]

A great deal of the motivation for these restricted languages – and a major influence on their phraseology – has come from the language of air traffic control, which presents international safety with its greatest challenge. Far more nations are forced to make routine daily communications with each other in relation to air transportation than ever occurs on the sea. Only a handful of nations are truly seafaring; but all nations are nowadays airborne. And the pace of change here has been truly phenomenal. In 1940, US air carriers were handling around 2 million passengers a year in about 350 planes; in 1950 the totals had grown to some 17 million in over 1,000 planes. In 2000 the number of passengers worldwide exceeded 1,650 million.[22]

The official use of English as the language of international aircraft control did not emerge until after the Second World War.

[21] Johnson (1993).
[22] Annual report of the International Civil Aviation Organization (2001).

Allied leaders organized a conference in Chicago in 1944 at which they laid the foundations for the post-war global civil aviation system, creating the International Civil Aviation Organization. Seven years later they agreed that English should be the international language of aviation when pilots and controllers speak different languages. This would have been the obvious choice for a lingua franca. The leaders of the Allies were English-speaking; the major aircraft manufacturers were English-speaking; and most of the post-war pilots in the West (largely ex-military personnel) were English-speaking.

The arguments in favour of a single language of air traffic control are obvious. It is safer if all pilots understand all conversations. Pilots who have a two-way radio are required to keep a listening watch at all times on the appropriate frequency. They listen not only to messages addressed to themselves, but also to messages being sent to and from other pilots in their neighbourhood. In this way they can learn about weather and traffic conditions from other pilots, without having to keep referring to air traffic control. Furthermore, if they hear an error in someone else's conversation, they can draw attention to it. If more than one language is being used, the risk of a breakdown in communication inevitably increases.

There have however been several cases where the case for bilingual air traffic control has been strongly argued, and sometimes this has led to a difficult political situation (such as the strike by pilots and air traffic controllers over a bilingual policy in Quebec, Canada, in 1976). Supporters of bilingual air traffic control stress the fact that not all pilots have a good command of English. They may have a poor pronunciation, which is made even more difficult for a controller to understand by the presence of background aircraft noise and the effects of stress on the voice. Pilots also may have difficulty understanding a controller, for the same reasons. Under such circumstances, it has been argued, it may actually be safer if both parties are allowed to communicate fluently with each other in a language they both understand well.

These arguments are still encountered in parts of the world where bilingual identity is critical, and two languages are officially used in certain localities (such as the use of French at Montreal). But in general the strength of the argument for a single language of air traffic control is not questioned, nor is the role of English. However, the issue is not simply to do with choosing one language; it is far more to do with moulding that language so that it is suitable for its purpose – economical and precise communication, to ensure safety at all times.

Even within a single language, terminology and phrasing need to be standardized, to avoid ambiguity, and great efforts have been made to develop such a system for English, widely called 'Airspeak'. Everyone knows – if only from the movies – that pilots do not talk in a normal way to air traffic control. They use a restricted vocabulary and a fixed set of sentence patterns which aim to express unambiguously all possible air situations. They include terms such as 'Roger', 'Wilco', and 'Mayday'; phrases such as 'Maintaining 2500 feet' and 'Runway in sight'; and the use of a phonetic alphabet to spell out codenames ('Alpha, Bravo, Charlie, Delta . . . ').[23]

Over 180 nations have adopted the recommendations of the International Civil Aviation Organization (ICAO) about English terminology. However, there is nothing mandatory about them (nor about Seaspeak, and other such systems). Even the US Federal Aviation Administration uses wording which differs from ICAO's in many instances. A proposal for a new international glossary has been discussed for some time. The problem is plain: it is relatively easy to set up a working party which will compile a single terminology for world use; the difficulty comes in persuading everyone to comply with it (which is likely to mean changing a country's traditional practice).

Under these circumstances, rather than try to impose a single Airspeak on everyone, some authorities think that it may be more satisfactory, in the long term, to work towards improving the quality of English used by air personnel. There are currently no agreed international standards for aviation English, or tests that all pilots have to take. And although most pilots' level of English is far greater than the level required by Airspeak norms, many would

---

[23] See, for example, Civil Aviation Authority (2002).

find it difficult to use English in any daily circumstance outside of that used in aircraft communication.

Arguments about safety involve many factors, and it is difficult to isolate one (such as language) and rely on it entirely. But there are some famous cases where the primary cause of the accident does seem to have been linguistic. In 1977, unclear English accents and terminology caused the collision between two Boeing 747s on the foggy runway at Tenerife – the worst disaster in aviation history. A KLM captain thought the Spanish controller had cleared him for take-off, whereas the controller had intended only to give departure instructions. In 1995, poor communication caused an American Airlines plane to crash at Cali, Colombia. An accident prevention study carried out by Boeing found that, in the decade 1982–1991, pilot–controller miscommunication contributed to at least 11 per cent of fatal crashes worldwide.

People have used cases of this kind to argue in support of bilingual air traffic control, or the use of a simpler auxiliary language such as Esperanto. But it seems likely that the problem of poor accents, background noise, and other variables would present difficulties, regardless of the language in use. In the meantime, English – with all its failings – remains the recommended language of international air travel.

Education

It follows from what has been said in this chapter that English is the medium of a great deal of the world's knowledge, especially in such areas as science and technology. And access to knowledge is the business of education. When we investigate why so many nations have in recent years made English an official language or chosen it as their chief foreign language in schools, one of the most important reasons is always educational – in the broadest sense. Black South African writer Harry Mashabela puts it like this:[24]

---

[24] Mashabela (1983: 17).

learning and using English will not only give us the much-needed uni-fying chord but will also land us into the exciting world of ideas; it will enable us to keep company with kings in the world of ideas and also make it possible for us to share the experiences of our own brothers in the world . . .

And Sridath Ramphal adds an anecdote:[25]

shortly after I became Secretary-General of the Commonwealth in 1975, I met Prime Minister Sirimavo Bandaranaike in Colombo and we talked of ways in which the Commonwealth Secretariat could help Sri Lanka. Her response was immediate and specific: 'Send us people to train our teachers to teach English as a foreign language'. My amazement must have showed, for the Prime Minister went on to explain that the policies her husband had put in place twenty years earlier to promote Sinhalese as the official language had succeeded so well that in the process Sri Lanka – so long the pearl of the English-speaking world in Asia – had in fact lost English, even as a second language save for the most educated Sri Lankans. Her concern was for development. Farmers in the field, she told me, could not read the instructions on bags of imported fertiliser – and manufacturers in the global market were not likely to print them in Sinhalese. Sri Lanka was losing its access to the world language of English. We did respond. I believe that today English is doing better as the second language in Sri Lanka.

Not everyone has viewed the arrival of the language in such a positive light, as we shall see in chapter 5; but the dominant view is certainly that a person is more likely to be in touch with the latest thinking and research in a subject by learning English than by learning any other language.

It is important to appreciate that the use of English does vary, in this respect. A 1980 study of the use of English in scientific pe-riodicals showed that 85 per cent of papers in biology and physics were being written in English at that time, whereas medical papers were some way behind (73 per cent), and papers in mathematics and chemistry further behind still (69 per cent and 67 per cent

---

[25] Ramphal (1996).

respectively).[26] However, all these areas had shown a significant increase in their use of English during the preceding fifteen years – over 30 per cent, in the case of chemistry, and over 40 per cent, in the case of medicine – and the figures twenty years further on would certainly be much higher. This can be seen even in a language-sensitive subject such as linguistics, where in 1995 nearly 90 per cent of the 1,500 papers listed in the journal *Linguistics Abstracts* were in English. In computer science, the proportion is even higher.

Since the 1960s, English has become the normal medium of instruction in higher education for many countries – and is increasingly used in several where the language has no official status. Some advanced courses in The Netherlands, for example, are widely taught in English. If most students are going to encounter English routinely in their monographs and periodicals, it is suggested – an argument which is particularly cogent in relation to the sciences – then it makes sense to teach advanced courses in that language, to better prepare them for that encounter. But these days there is also a strong lingua franca argument: the pressure to use English has grown as universities and colleges have increasingly welcomed foreign students, and lecturers have found themselves faced with mixed-language audiences.

The English language teaching (ELT) business has become one of the major growth industries around the world in the past half-century. However, its relevance to the growth of English as a world language goes back much further. In the final quarter of the eighteenth century, we find several examples of English grammars, such as Lindley Murray's, being translated into other languages.[27] An illustration of the scale of the development in modern times can be seen from the work of The British Council, which in 2002 had a network of offices in 109 countries promoting cultural, educational and technical cooperation. In 1995–6, for example, over 400,000 candidates worldwide sat English language examinations administered by the Council, over half of these being examinations in English as a foreign language. At any one time during that year, there were 120,000 students learning

---

[26] Large (1983: 18).   [27] Tieken-Boon van Ostade (1996).

English and other skills through the medium of English in Council teaching centres. The figures have steadily grown since then. With thousands of other schools and centres worldwide now also devoted to English-language teaching, the Council estimated that the new millennium would see over 1,000 million people learning English.[28]

In a 1995 global consultation exercise initiated by *English 2000*, a British Council project, people professionally involved in ELT in some ninety countries were asked to react to a series of statements concerning the role and future of the English language.[29] Responses used a 5-point scale from 'strongly agree' to 'strongly disagree'. Nearly 1,400 questionnaires were returned. One of the statements was: 'The global market for English language teaching and learning will increase over the next 25 years.' Over 93 per cent agreed or strongly agreed. A particular growth area is central and eastern Europe, and the countries of the former Soviet Union, where it is thought that over 10 per cent of the population – some 50 million in all – are now learning English.

Certain other statements in the Council questionnaire were also given an unequivocal response. They included:

- English will retain its role as the dominant language in world media and communications. 94 per cent agreed or strongly agreed.
- English is essential for progress as it will provide the main means of access to high-tech communication and information over the next twenty-five years. 95 per cent agreed or strongly agreed.
- English will remain the world's language for international communication for the next twenty-five years. 96 per cent agreed or strongly agreed.

Exercises of this kind have no clear predictive value, but they do provide a useful glimpse of the way specialists are thinking in the world market-place, and when identical opinions are expressed from so many countries they undoubtedly help to confirm the picture of English emerging as a global language.

[28] British Council (1997).   [29] British Council (1995).

Communications

If a language is a truly international medium, it is going to be most apparent in those services which deal directly with the task of communication – the postal and telephone systems and the electronic networks. Information about the use of English in these domains is not easy to come by, however. No one monitors the language in which we write our letters; there is no one noting the language we use when we talk on the phone. Only on the Internet, where messages and data can be left for indefinite periods of time, is it possible to develop an idea of how much of the world's everyday communications (at least, between computer-owners) is actually in English.

There are various indirect methods of calculation, of course. We can draw up a list of those countries where English has special status (see chapter 2), and look at the pieces of mail sent, or the number of telephone calls made. Data of this kind are available, though hedged in with many qualifications. For example, using the information compiled in the 2002 Britannica *Yearbook*,[30] it transpires that about 63 per cent of the world's mail in 2001 was being handled by English-status countries. However, information is not available for thirty-two countries, and those countries which have provided totals arrived at them in a variety of ways.

One fact is plain: the amount of mail sent through just the US postal system that year (some 197 thousand million pieces) was larger than the total for all the non-English-speaking countries put together. Indeed, if the USA is matched against **all** other countries, it accounts for nearly half of the world's volume of postal traffic. Even if we assume that the proportion of the US population which speaks other languages (about 15 per cent) never writes in English, we must still conclude that 40 per cent of the world's mail is in English, from the USA alone.

A widely quoted statistic is that three-quarters of the world's mail is in English. It is certainly possible to arrive at this figure if we make guesses about the number of people in different countries who are involved in organizations which use English as an official

[30] *Encyclopaedia Britannica* (2002: 850ff.).

114

language, or which rely on English for correspondence. When scientists from any country write to each other, for example, the language they use is almost always going to be English. The figures for international mail are likely to reflect those for international associations cited above, where again English is widespread. But there are no precise calculations.

Another widely quoted statistic is that about 80 per cent of the world's electronically stored information is currently in English. Figures of this kind relate to two kinds of data: information stored privately by individual firms and organizations, such as commercial businesses, libraries and security forces; and information made available through the Internet, whether for sending and receiving electronic mail, participating in discussion groups, or providing and accessing databases and data pages. Statistics of this kind have to be cautiously interpreted. They seem to be little more than extrapolations from computer sales and distribution patterns – and thus simply reflect the pioneering role of the USA in developing and marketing computational hardware and software. In particular, given the American origins of the Internet (as ARPANET, the Advanced Research Projects Agency network devised in the late 1960s), it is not surprising that most Internet hosts – 64 per cent, according to a *Business Week* survey[31] – are to be found in the USA. A further 12.7 per cent were thought to be in other English-speaking countries. But there is no easy way of predicting the language of Internet users or documents from the location of their hosts.

It is important for the theme of this book to see how English came to have such a dominant position on the Internet.[32] ARPANET was conceived as a decentralized national network, its aim being to link important American academic and government institutions in a way which would survive local damage in the event of a major war. Its language was, accordingly, English; and when people in other countries began to form links with this

---

[31] Business Week (1996).
[32] This topic receives a fuller treatment in Crystal (2001: chapter 7). A NUA Internet Survey in 2002, <www.nua.ie>, estimates 544.2 million world users online, with a third (181 million) in the USA and Canada; 46% are in English-speaking countries.

network, it proved essential for them to use English. The dominance of this language was then reinforced when the service was opened up in the 1980s to private and commercial organizations, most of which were (for the reasons given earlier in this chapter) already communicating chiefly in English.

There was also a technical reason underpinning the position of the language at this time. The first protocols devised to carry data on the Net were developed for the English alphabet, using a character set (called Latin 1) which had no diacritical marks and which was transmitted in a 7-bit ASCII code. An 8-bit code and a character set including diacritics (Latin 2) later became available, and more sophisticated protocols were devised with multilingualism in mind, but major problems have hindered their international implementation in a standardized way. Unicode, using a 16-bit code, allowed the representation of nearly 50,000 characters (version 3, rising to over 94,000 in version 3.1), but even this is not enough to handle the characters in all the world's languages, which have been estimated at over 170,000.[33] There are problems of data representation and manipulation (especially involving the selection, encoding, and conversion of character sets), data display (handling such issues as the direction of a writing system, or the mapping of character codes into an appropriate range of images on screen), and data input (such as the use of different keyboard layouts and techniques). Several *ad hoc* solutions have been devised, but *ad hoc* solutions bring with them problems of compatibility, and this limits the ability of the World Wide Web to be truly interoperable – that is, enabling all servers and clients to communicate intelligently with each other, whatever the data source.

Most browsers are still unable to handle multilingual data presentation. More than just diacritics is involved, as is evident from a consideration of such writing systems as Arabic, Chinese, Korean, Thai and Hindi, some of which require very large character sets. More than alphabetic text is involved: there are difficulties in handling conventions to do with money, dates, measurements, and other types of special setting which need to be anticipated. At

---

[33] Goundry (2001). The Unicode site is at <www.unicode.org>.

present a truly multilingual World Wide Web remains a long-term goal – a Web where end users can expect to input data using their language of choice in a routine way, and can expect any server to receive and display the data without problems.[34]

In the meantime, English continues to be the chief lingua franca of the Internet – a position which during the 1990s began to be acknowledged in the popular media. For example, in April 1996 *The New York Times* carried an article by Michael Specter headed 'World, Wide, Web: 3 English Words', in which the role of English was highlighted:[35]

To study molecular genetics, all you need to get into the Harvard University Library, or the medical library at Sweden's Karolinska Institute, is a phone line and a computer.

And, it turns out, a solid command of the English language. Because whether you are a French intellectual pursuing the cutting edge of international film theory, a Japanese paleobotanist curious about a newly discovered set of primordial fossils, or an American teen-ager concerned about Magic Johnson's jump shot, the Internet and World Wide Web really only work as great unifiers if you speak English.

Specter concludes: 'if you want to take full advantage of the Internet there is only one way to do it: learn English, which has more than ever become America's greatest and most effective export'. The article goes on to consider the international consequences of this situation – and in particular some of the negative ones. A sub-heading reads: 'A force for global unity' – adding in ironic parentheses '(if you know the language)'. Specter quotes Anatoly Voronov, the director of Glasnet, an Internet provider in Russia:

It is the ultimate act of intellectual colonialism. The product comes from America so we must either adapt to English or stop using it. That is the right of business. But if you are talking about a technology that is supposed to open the world to hundreds of millions of people you are joking. This just makes the world into new sorts of haves and have nots.

[34] The Babel site, an Alis Technologies/Internet Society joint project to internationalize the Internet, is a good source of information on current developments: <http://babel.alis.com:8080>.
[35] Specter (1996).

Is it a serious possibility – that unless you are able to use English, you will be unable to take advantage of the intellectual power which the Internet provides? Does the Net have the power to divide people into two classes of citizen – Internet literates and illiterates? Is the 'intellectual ghetto' a real prospect?

The problem seems large now, but it is probably only temporary. Anatoly Voronov comments that 'it is far easier for a Russian language speaker with a computer to download the works of Dostoyevsky translated into English to read than it is for him to get the original in his own language'. This is a pity. But the speed with which the Net is growing and adapting is so great that it is unlikely that the situation will obtain for long. Eventually, someone will find it worthwhile to put Dostoyevsky in Russian on the Net. It may well be happening already. As the demand for material in other languages grows, so will the supply. None of this will remove the dominance of English on the Net, but it will reduce the risk of international intellectual ghettoes. That risk, in any case, is less to do with linguistics than it is with economics, education, and technology: can people afford to buy computers? do they know how to use them? does their country have the necessary infrastructure? is finance available for database compilation? Computer illiteracy is more the result of lack of money than lack of English.

Is it possible to provide evidence to test impressions of this kind about the strength of English? Can the 80 per cent claim referred to above be substantiated? One technique is to carry out a series of searches on a particular host to see how many of the items retrieved are in English. For example, a Netscape search made in July 1996 on the World Wide Web using Lycos established that all of the references made to *tritium* were in English – as we might expect for such an unequivocably scientific subject. A search for information about a cultural item, *orchestras*, found only one record in the first 100 documents in a language other than English. Interestingly, several orchestras from non-English-status countries had ensured that their Web page was in English – for example, the Shanghai National Music Orchestra (China) and the Lahti Symphony Orchestra (Finland). Also of interest was the corresponding search carried out on the word for *orchestra* in other languages: *orchestre* (French) produced 39 English entries out of the first 100; *Orchester* (German) produced 34 out of 76 (the total number of records found); and *orquesta* (Spanish) produced 35 out of 78. It is quite common to see a message attached to a foreign-language record: 'These pages are also available in English'. It is unusual to see the corresponding foreign-language message attached to an English page.

Carrying out a series of random searches in this way, for both English-language and other-language keywords, during the 1990s one did consistently end up with a figure of about 80 per cent. However, the proportion is becoming much less, as more people from more countries come on-line, and the changes have been very rapid, in view of the remarkable growth in Internet use. From a million users in 1990, estimates by the Internet Society suggested there were 20 million users in 1993, and over 40 million by the end of 1995, with growth continuing at a rate of about 10 per cent a month in 1996. Web users at that time were represented in some 90 countries, and e-mail facilities were available in a further 70 countries. The 2002 NUA survey reported on p. 115 estimates 544 million users distributed across 201 territories. The number of non-English language users on the Internet is thus growing all the time. Already in 1999 predictions were being made that in the early 2000s non-English users would exceed English users, and estimates appearing in 2002 suggest that this may already have happened.[36] Moreover, the shift has hardly begun, given that so few people from Latin America and Africa are yet online: the NUA survey estimates usage in Latin America and the Caribbean to be only 25.33 million in 2000–1, and in Africa to be a tiny 4.15 million. It seems likely that Internet usage will in due course reflect the world's linguistic demographics, with English users hovering around 30 per cent (see p. 69). On the other hand, the head start English has had means that there is more high-quality content on the Web in English than in other languages, so that even if the proportion of English-language sites

[36] For example, Dillon (1999), reporting research by Computer Economics Inc. which predicted a non-English majority by 2002 and English down to 40% by 2005. A 2002 survey by <global-reach.biz> finds English down to 40% already. For a further example of the shift in media opinion, see Wallraff (2000).

falls soon, the number of hits on those sites (i.e. individuals calling up specific Web addresses) may remain disproportionately high for some time.

A particularly interesting effect of the Internet has been its role in relation to minority and endangered languages. These languages are finding that the Net gives them a louder and cheaper voice than is available through such traditional media as radio, and Websites and chatgroups ('virtual speech communities') are now common in, for example Galician, Basque, Irish Gaelic, Breton and Welsh. Well over 1000 languages can be found on the Internet in 2002, notwithstanding the technical difficulties referred to above.[37] This is good news for those worried by the global trend in language loss (p. 20), but it is also good news for those concerned that global intelligibility should not lose out to local identity. On the Net, all languages are as equal as their users wish to make them, and English emerges as an alternative rather than a threat.

The right place at the right time

What are we to conclude, after this wide-ranging review of the way English has come to be used in the modern world? Is there a common theme which can help us explain the remarkable growth of this language? The evidence of this chapter, and that of chapter 3, is that it is a language which has repeatedly found itself in the right place at the right time (p. 78).

In the seventeenth and eighteenth centuries English was the language of the leading colonial nation – Britain. In the eighteenth and nineteenth centuries it was the language of the leader of the industrial revolution – also Britain. In the late nineteenth century and the early twentieth it was the language of the leading economic power – the USA. As a result, when new technologies brought new linguistic opportunities, English emerged as a first-rank language in industries which affected all aspects of society – the press, advertising, broadcasting, motion pictures, sound recording, transport and communications. At the same time, the

[37] See the review in Crystal (2000: chapter 7).

world was forging fresh networks of international alliances, and there emerged an unprecedented need for a lingua franca. Here too, there was a clear first choice. During the first half of the twentieth century English gradually became a leading language of international political, academic, and community meetings.

By the 1960s, the pre-eminence of the language was established, but it could not at that time have been described as a genuine world language, in the sense described in chapter 1. Since then, however, two events have together ensured its global status. The first was the movement towards political independence, out of which English emerged as a language with special status in several new countries. In most of these, the role of English had come to be so fundamental that no other language could compete, when the moment of independence arrived. The other event was the electronic revolution, where here too English was in the right place (the USA) at the right time (the 1970s).

The development of twentieth-century computers has been almost entirely an American affair. As Michael Specter puts it, in his *New York Times* article: 'The Internet started in the United States, and the computer hackers whose reality has always been virtual are almost all Americans. By the time the net spread, its linguistic patterns – like its principal architecture and best software – were all Made in the USA.' Although computer languages are not like natural languages, being very restricted, they have inevitably been greatly influenced by the mother tongue of the programmers – and this has largely been English. The first computer operating systems automatically used English vocabulary and syntax, as can be seen in such instructions as 'Press any key when ready' and 'Volume in Drive B has no label'. These are examples from MS (Microsoft) DOS, the system developed in 1977 by US computer entrepreneur Bill Gates, and which was adopted by IBM in 1981 for its range of computers. The more recent operating systems, replacing DOS, have displayed English influence too, though alternatives in a few other languages are now available (where the commercial advantages have justified the development costs, as in French and German). And it seems likely that the influence of English will remain, as programs become increasingly sophisticated and allow users to make more natural-sounding commands.

It is difficult to predict the future, with something so dynamic as the Internet. In a few generations' time, the Net will not be like anything we know today. Automatic speech synthesis and recognition will be routine, and (notwithstanding the difficulties described on p. 27) more use will be made of automatic translation. The arrival of high-quality immediate translation facilities will have a major impact on the use of English (or any lingua franca) on the Net; but these are a long way off. For the near future, it is difficult to foresee any developments which could eliminate the significant role of English on the information superhighway. The biggest potential setback to English as a global language, it has been said with more than a little irony, would have taken place a generation ago – if Bill Gates had grown up speaking Chinese.

5

The future of global English

After a while, any account of the social history of English, such as the one recounted in chapters 3 and 4, starts to repeat itself. Under each heading, the narrative identifies a major domain of modern society, puts it in a historical perspective, then discusses the extent to which it now uses or depends upon English. The overwhelming impression, after such an exercise, must be that the language is alive and well, and that its global future is assured.

But linguistic history shows us repeatedly that it is wise to be cautious, when making predictions about the future of a language. If, in the Middle Ages, you had dared to predict the death of Latin as the language of education, people would have laughed in your face – as they would, in the eighteenth century, if you had suggested that any language other than French could be a future norm of polite society. A week may be a long time in politics; but a century is a short time in linguistics.

In speculating about the future of English as a world language, therefore, we need to pay careful attention to indications which seem to go against the general trend. And we need to ask, in broad terms: What kinds of development could impede the future growth of English? It will then be possible to arrive at a balanced conclusion.

Several possibilities can be envisaged. A significant change in the balance of power – whether political, economic, technological or cultural (p. 10) – could affect the standing of other languages so that they become increasingly attractive, and begin to take over functions currently assumed by English. Political factors might make groups of people within a country, or even whole countries or groups of countries, antagonistic to English. Pressures arising out of the need to express community identity might disrupt the ability of English to function as a global language. Here, the chief scenario envisaged is one where the language fragments into mutually unintelligible varieties, in much the way that vulgar Latin did a millennium ago. This chapter deals with the issues raised by these possibilities.

The rejection of English

We begin with the situation where the people of a country feel so antagonistic or ambivalent about English that they reject the option to give English a privileged status, either as an official language or as a foreign language. If several countries were to begin thinking in this way, there could in due course be a pendulum swing which would render the claim of global status less credible. The chief reasons for such antipathy were briefly discussed in chapter 1, when we began our inquiry into the general nature of a global language. We may apply this reasoning now, in relation to the particular case of English.

It is inevitable that, in a post-colonial era, there should be a strong reaction against continuing to use the language of the former colonial power, and in favour of promoting the indigenous languages. As the then president of Kenya, Jomo Kenyatta, said in 1974, 'The basis of any independent government is a national language, and we can no longer continue aping our former colonizers.' Gandhi, writing in 1908, puts the point more emotively:[1]

To give millions a knowledge of English is to enslave them . . . Is it not a painful thing that, if I want to go to a court of justice, I must employ the English language as a medium; that, when I became a Barrister, I may not speak my mother-tongue, and that someone else should have to translate to me from my own language? Is this not absolutely absurd? Is it not a sign of slavery?

[1] Gandhi (1958: 5).

The Kenyan author, Ngũgĩ wa Thiong'o, who chose to reject English as the medium of expression for his work in favour of Gikuyu and Kiswahili, is equally forceful in his book *Decolonising the mind*:[2]

I am lamenting a neo-colonial situation which has meant the European bourgeoisie once again stealing our talents and geniuses as they have stolen our economies. In the eighteenth and nineteenth centuries Europe stole art treasures from Africa to decorate their houses and museums; in the twentieth century Europe is stealing the treasures of the mind to enrich their languages and cultures. Africa needs back its economy, its politics, its culture, its languages and all its patriotic writers.

The arguments are all to do with identity, and with language as the most immediate and universal symbol of that identity. People have a natural wish to use their own mother-tongue, to see it survive and grow, and they do not take kindly when the language of another culture is imposed on them. Despite the acknowledged values which the language of that culture can bring, the fact remains that English has an unhappy colonial resonance in the minds of many, and a history where local languages could easily be treated with contempt. Here is another extract from *Decolonising the mind*, in which Ngũgĩ wa Thiong'o remembers his schooldays:[3]

English became the language of my formal education. In Kenya, English became more than a language: it was *the* language, and all the others had to bow before it in deference.

Thus one of the most humiliating experiences was to be caught speaking Gikuyu in the vicinity of the school. The culprit was given corporal punishment – three to five strokes of the cane on bare buttocks – or was made to carry a metal plate around the neck with inscriptions such as I AM STUPID or I AM A DONKEY.

It is not difficult to see how antagonism to English can grow, with such memories. Equally, it is easy to see how ambivalence can grow. Many writers in the countries of the outer circle (p. 60)

---

[2] Ngũgĩ wa Thiong'o (1986: xii).   [3] Ibid., 11.

see themselves as facing a dilemma: if they write in English, their work will have the chance of reaching a worldwide audience; but to write in English may mean sacrificing their cultural identity. The dilemma can be partially resolved, as we shall see (p. 183).

On the whole, the former colonies of the British Empire have stayed with English (see the list at the end of chapter 2), but there are some famous instances of distancing or rejection. In Tanzania, English was jointly official with Swahili until 1967 (thereafter, Swahili became the sole national language); in Malaysia, the National Language Act of 1967 disestablished English as a joint official language, giving sole status to Malay. On the other hand, English has begun to increase its prestige in several countries which were formerly part of other empires, and where it has no unpalatable colonial associations. In 1996, for example, Algeria (a former French colony) opted to make English its chief foreign language in schools, replacing French. And it is interesting to note that, in the excited debates surrounding the proposed creation of the state of Padania in Northern Italy, also in 1996, some secessionists were citing English as a more acceptable candidate for a lingua franca than standard Italian.

There are also economic arguments which might persuade a country to reduce its investment in the English language. A country might see its economic future as operating more on a regional than a global level, and thus devote extra resources to fostering a local lingua franca. The Spanish-speaking countries of Latin America could throw their weight behind Spanish, for example, or the countries of North Africa behind Arabic. Hindi, Russian, and German are other examples of languages which have a traditional presence within a number of geographically adjacent countries. The immediate benefits of using a language already well established in the locality could outweigh, in their mind, the longer-term benefits of introducing English. They might want no part in a global economic village, or dismiss the possibility as a pipe-dream. The current debate on the merits and demerits of European economic union suggests that the benefits are not always clear.[4]

[4] Alternative economic scenarios are explored by Graddol (1998).

The need for intelligibility and the need for identity often pull people – and countries – in opposing directions. The former motivates the learning of an international language, with English the first choice in most cases; the latter motivates the promotion of ethnic language and culture. Conflict is the common consequence when either position is promoted insensitively. There are ways of avoiding such conflict, of course, notably in the promotion of bilingual or multilingual policies, which enable people both 'to have their cake and eat it'. But bilingual policies are expensive to resource, in both time and money, and they require a climate of cooperation which for historical reasons often does not exist.

Any decision to reject English has important consequences for the identity of a nation, and it can cause emotional ripples (both sympathetic and antagonistic) around the English-speaking world; but there have been very few such rejections of English to date, and the populations in the countries which have done so are sufficiently small that even in total there has been no noticeable impact on the status of the English language as a whole. There is, however, one country where, on grounds of population-size alone, a major change in the sociolinguistic situation could turn ripples into waves. That is the USA.

Contrasting attitudes: the US situation

Given that the USA has come to be the dominant element in so many of the domains identified in earlier chapters, the future status of English must be bound up to some extent with the future of that country. So much of the power which has fuelled the growth of the English language during the twentieth century has stemmed from America. We have already noted that the country contains nearly four times as many mother-tongue speakers of English as any other nation. It has been more involved with international developments in twentieth-century technology than any other nation. It is in control of the new industrial (that is, electronic) revolution. And it exercises a greater influence on the way English is developing worldwide than does any other regional variety – often, of course, to the discomfiture of people in the UK, Australia, New Zealand, Canada and South Africa, who regularly express worries in their national presses about the onslaught of 'Americanisms'.

As we have seen in chapter 1, there is the closest of links between language and power. If anything were to disestablish the military or economic power of the USA, there would be inevitable consequences for the global status of the language. The millions of people learning English in order to have access to this power would begin to look elsewhere, and (assuming the new political magnet used a language other than English) they would quickly acquire new language loyalties. It is unlikely that a corresponding loss of power in any other country would have such a serious effect. Even if, for example, the entire English-speaking population of Canada decided to switch to French, or the entire English-speaking population of South Africa opted to speak Afrikaans, the implications for English as a world language would be minor. As can be seen from the listing in chapter 2, relatively small numbers of people would be involved.

No one has suggested that the power of the USA is seriously at risk from external forces, as we begin the new millennium; the International Institute for Strategic Studies (in *The military balance 1996–7*) reports that the USA still has by far the most powerful conventional armed forces in the world and is the largest arms producer. But during the 1990s increasing attention came to be focused on a domestic debate in which, according to one set of arguments, there are internal forces threatening the country's future unity. As we have seen in chapter 2 (p. 36), some analysts consider the English language to have been an important factor in maintaining mutual intelligibility and American unity in the face of the immigration explosion which more than tripled the US population after 1900. For those who take this view, the contemporary movement among some immigrant populations to maintain their original cultural identity through safeguarding their mother tongues is – given the large numbers involved – a matter of some consequence. What has emerged is a conflict between the demands of intelligibility and identity (of the kind outlined in chapter 1), and one outcome has been the 'official English' movement. Although the various arguments are in many ways unique to the USA, given the large numbers of people and languages involved, and relating as they do to the rights of individuals as enshrined in the US Constitution, they need to be carefully noted by people in other countries, for ethnic minority and immigrant populations – and thus the competing pressures of identity preservation vs. assimilation – are everywhere. Although there is no official-language movement in Britain, for example, it is not impossible to imagine an analogous situation developing there, as well as in Australia, where immigration trends in recent years have been especially dramatic, and where in the 1990s the country's attitude towards Asian immigrants emerged again as a political issue. A summary of the main issues is therefore of some relevance, in a book dealing with the future of global English.[5]

Why, in a country where over 95 per cent of the population speak English, should there be a movement to make English official? People do not start making a case for a language to be made official until they feel they need to; and the circumstances in which they need to are usually very clear. As already mentioned (p. 84), the typical scenario is one where a language has come to be threatened by the emergence of a more dominant language. It may take a long time for people who speak the threatened language to respond: in the case of Welsh, the reversal of several hundred years of English domination has begun to show real results only recently, starting with the Welsh Language Act of 1967. Similar movements can be seen in Ireland, Hawaii, New Zealand, and Quebec. Inevitably, in such cases, there is a secondary reaction, with English-users finding themselves – often for the first time – on the defensive (in relation to such matters as job applications, where bilingualism may be advantageous), and insisting that the status of English be guaranteed. But in a country where the language is already so dominant, and its position for so long taken for granted, why should the question of its official status arise at all?

Before going into the reasons, it should be mentioned that the positions for and against 'official English' have been argued

---

[5] For the sociolinguistic situation in contemporary USA, see Herriman and Burnaby (1996: chapter 6). For the US-English position, see <www.us-english.org>. For a critique of the English-Only position, see Nunberg (1999).

with varying amounts of moderation and extremism, and that several views are possible on each side. On the pro-official side, no fewer than three bills came before the House of Representatives in January–February 1995, all sponsored by Republicans (but with varying amounts of inter-party support), expressing different attitudes and recommendations about the use and status of other languages. The most moderate of these (HR 123, sponsored by Representative Bill Emerson), outlined below, saw itself partly as a means of empowering immigrants by giving them greater opportunities to acquire English. Considerably more radical was HR 739, sponsored by Representative Toby Roth, which allowed for fewer exceptions in the official use of other languages, and repealed the 1965 Act providing for bilingual education and bilingual ballots. More restrictive still was HR 1005, sponsored by Representative Pete King, which allowed for even fewer exceptions in the use of other languages. The latter two proposals made little political progress; but HR 123 received the support of US English, the country's leading organization campaigning for official English, and it was this bill which eventually went to a vote, in August 1996, being passed by the House of Representatives (under the name of the Bill Emerson English Language Empowerment Act) by 259 to 169. However, pressure of time in a presidential election year did not allow the bill to reach the Senate, and it remains to be seen how the issue will fare in future Congresses.

This summary of the main clauses of the Emerson bill is based on the bill as presented to the House on 4 January 1995. It does not include any amendments introduced at the committee stage in July 1996 or thereafter.

(1) the United States is comprised of individuals and groups from diverse ethnic, cultural, and linguistic backgrounds;

(2) the United States has benefited and continues to benefit from this rich diversity;

(3) throughout the history of the Nation, the common thread binding those of differing backgrounds has been a common language;

(4) in order to preserve unity in diversity, and to prevent division along linguistic lines, the United States should maintain a language common to all people;

(5) English has historically been the common language and the language of opportunity in the United States;

(6) the purpose of this Act is to help immigrants better assimilate and take full advantage of economic and occupational opportunities in the United States;

(7) by learning the English language, immigrants will be empowered with the language skills and literacy necessary to become responsible citizens and productive workers in the United States;

(8) the use of a single common language in the conduct of the Government's official business will promote efficiency and fairness to all people;

(9) English should be recognized in law as the language of official business of the Government; and

(10) any monetary savings derived from the enactment of this Act should be used for the teaching of the non-English speaking immigrants the English language.

In a series of further clauses, it was made clear that 'official business' meant 'those governmental actions, documents, or policies which are enforceable with the full weight and authority of the Government' – this would include all public records, legislation, regulations, hearings, official ceremonies, and public meetings. The bill allowed the use of languages other than English in such cases as public health and safety services, the teaching of foreign languages, policies necessary for international relations and trade, and actions that protect the rights of people involved in judicial proceedings. Private businesses were not affected. The bill also stated that it was not its purpose 'to discriminate against or restrict the rights of any individual' or 'to discourage or prevent the use of languages other than English in any nonofficial capacity'.

There are also several positions on the anti-official side, though here it is not so easy to make generalizations. To begin with, there are many cultural perspectives, as we would expect from a population which includes, on the one hand, a major Hispanic group of over 28 millions (according to the 2000 census) and, on the other, a range of ethnic groups some of whose members number only a few thousand. Over 18 million claimed to speak a language other than English or Spanish in the home, in that census, with over 300 languages involved. Also, there is no single authoritative source of statement to refer to, but many organizations, each of which has its own political agenda. The observations below, accordingly, will not necessarily be endorsed by everyone who opposes official English legislation. They are paraphrases of views expressed in various policy statements, alternative proposals, and press articles or letters. But the points can be used in aggregate to spell out the case for opposition.

A wide range of arguments is used by each side in support of its case.

- *The political argument: for*   Pro-official supporters see in the emergence of major immigrant groups, and the support for immigrant language programmes, the seeds of separatism, and the eventual dissolution of the unity which is reflected in the very name of the United States and its motto (*E pluribus unum*, 'One out of many'). They look fearfully at the language-inspired separatist movement in nearby Quebec, which came close to success in 1995, and draw attention to the emergence of incendiary separatist attitudes such as are expressed by the Chicano Movement of Aztlan (MECha) or by the University of California student publication, *Voz Fronteriza* ('Voice of the frontier'), where writers envisage large tracts of the US south-west as one day returning to Hispanic (Mexicano) control. The term 'official Spanish' is increasingly encountered, in this connection. The fact that there is a linguistic dimension to the conflicts which destroyed former Yugoslavia is also sometimes cited as an example of the dangers lurking beneath the surface of a multilingual community: Speaker of the House Newt Gingrich, for example, participating in the debate on the Emerson bill, was one influential voice which referred to the perils of US 'Balkanization'.

From this point of view, English is viewed, according to one pro-official columnist in 1995, as a social adhesive – as a linguistic glue which guarantees political unity. According to another, the language has been the basis of social stability in the USA, and any threat to this stabilizing influence would lead to the growth of 'countries within a country' – linguistic ghettos which would discourage contact between groups and slow down the process of socialization. Attention is drawn to the size of the possible rift, especially in relation to the use of Spanish, with the US Census Bureau predicting more Hispanics than African-Americans in the USA by the year 2010, and a Hispanic population of over 80 million by 2050.

• *The political argument: against*   Anti-official supporters maintain that an official English bill is unnecessary – that the fears have been wildly exaggerated, there is no risk of disunity, and no danger of Babel. They argue that most immigrants are assimilating nicely – certainly by the second generation – and that the natural course of events will eventually produce a new social balance, without any need for legislation. There is no more need to make English official now, it is suggested, than there was at the time of the Revolution, when Dutch and German were for a while spoken by substantial numbers. The natural urge that people have to succeed will provide the required motivation for the learning of English. A common observation, they point out, is that first-generation immigrant parents actually find it harder to persuade their children to learn their language of origin than to learn English. It is felt that English could not possibly be in danger, in any case, when over 95 per cent of the population speak it 'well' or 'very well'. It is the other languages which are actually in danger.

Many accordingly hold the view that the official English bill is an unwarranted federal intrusion into self-expression, violating cultural pluralism, and – insofar as it is perceived as a policy intended to limit and control minorities – increasing the chances that communities would divide along ethnic lines. Even if English were made official, the argument continues, the use of a common language does not guarantee ethnic harmony. A community can be torn apart on racial, religious, political, or other grounds, even when both sides are united by a single language (see p. 16). There are evidently bigger issues in the world than linguistic ones, and this is reflected in some of the descriptors used by those most violently opposed to the 'official English' proposals, such as 'elitist', 'racist', 'anti-immigrant' and 'anti-Hispanic'.

- *The socio-economic argument: for*   Pro-official supporters maintain that, at a time when there is considerable competition for
limited funds, an expensive multilingual support policy is unde-
sirable. It is not as if there is just a single alternative language which
is in need of protection (as in the case of Canada): there are well
over 300 languages to be taken into account. They point out that
no country could afford a language policy which tried to give official protection to so many languages. The Canadian situation,
dealing with just two languages, cost that country nearly $7,000
million dollars in the decade from 1980 to 1990. The USA, with
ten times the population, and many more languages, would have
to find some multiple of that total each year, depending on how
many languages were selected for support.

   The problem of selection is thought to be particularly serious.
Pro-official supporters draw attention to the difficulty of saying
that a language can receive official recognition only after it reaches
a certain point of growth. If 5 million were chosen as the cut-off
point, for example, it would be inevitable that people who spoke
languages which were just a little short of that figure would claim
that the division was unfair. Some commentators therefore argue
that no principled selection is possible, and that the country is in an
all-or-none situation. If 'all': any foreign-language groups with a
tiny number of speakers would be able to claim official support –
but the country would soon go bankrupt, if it adopted such a
policy. The only alternative, this line of argument concludes, is
to support 'none' – other than the language of the vast majority,
English.

   It is also argued that the provision of alternative language services (such as the option of taking a driving test in a range of different languages) is highly wasteful of resources, because they are
so little used. One of the main themes of the leading pro-English
organization in the USA, US English, is to draw attention to cases
of this kind. For example, it cites the fact that in 1994 the Internal
Revenue Service distributed half a million forms and instruction
booklets in Spanish, but only 718 were returned. It expresses
concern about the cost of a language policy in which, for instance, in 2002 California was offering licence exams to drivers in
thirty-three different languages. It concludes that a better return

for money would come from spending it elsewhere: in improving the English-language abilities of immigrants to the USA. There is an important issue of empowerment here: pro-official supporters argue that educational programmes in the immigrant's mother tongue are no real help, because they eliminate the incentive for immigrants to learn English, and this keeps them in low-paid jobs. Official status, it is asserted, would help to safeguard English as the language of opportunity. There would also be enormous savings in efficiency, both at national and local levels, it is suggested, if everyone had the competence and confidence to rely on English as their medium of communication in official contexts. This would also ensure that everyone would understand road signs, safety regulations at work, medicinal instructions, environmental hazard warnings, and the like. If it is possible for someone to have such a poor knowledge of English that they have to take a driving exam in another language, the argument concludes, it is improbable that they will be able to cope with the English-language demands placed upon them by the multiplicity of road-side instructions.

• *The socio-economic argument: against*   Anti-official supporters doubt whether government time and money would really be saved, given the cost and complexity of introducing the new law. In particular, they question whether the legislation could possibly be enforced, and point to the difficulties of giving a precise definition to the notion of 'official', in relation to language, and of making a clear and consistent distinction between 'public' and 'private' discourse. For example, would a march in support of some minority issue be a public or private event, and would it be permitted to carry banners in languages other than English? The fear is that the public domain will gradually erode the private one, ultimately threatening freedom of speech. Especially in a country where there is a great readiness to use the courts to solve disputes, the new law would, it is felt, cause greater complications than it would solve, and would probably be more expensive to implement and maintain. It might actually end up being honoured more in the breach than in the observance, with the legislation proving inadequate to cope with the realities of a highly complex and dynamic social situation. An important complication is that any new layer of federal control would also have to be implemented alongside the individual laws enacted by several states (twenty-seven by 2002), which already display a great deal of variation.

The 'all-or-nothing' view of language support is also hotly contested, using the following line of reasoning. There may indeed be no principled way of drawing a line between one group of languages and another, but it does not follow from this that nothing should be done to help those who speak the more widely used languages, where relatively large numbers of people would benefit from receiving a modicum of support in their mother tongue. The fields of health and safety, such as those cited above, provide a good example of areas where much more could be done than is available at present. Some commentators have drawn attention to the different situation in other countries which have high immigrant populations. In Germany, for example, pharmaceutical companies have to provide instruction labels in five *Gastarbeiter* (immigrant 'guest-worker') languages: Turkish, Italian, Spanish, Serbo-Croatian, and Greek. They are not required to carry such labels in the several other languages currently found in Germany, such as Russian and Polish. In this view, to introduce a policy banning all such labels on the grounds that some languages cannot be represented is felt to be absurd. It is thought to be common sense to provide safety instructions on medicine bottles in as many languages as is practicable, to minimize the risk to as many people as possible. It is not feasible to help everyone who has difficulty with English, but it is not acceptable to conclude from this that the government should therefore help none of them.

Even though the moderate official-English position maintains that it has no intention of harming ethnic identity or the natural growth of languages other than English, anti-official supporters claim that the withdrawal of resources and the fresh focus on English is bound to harm the provision of services in these languages, even in areas which are supposed to be protected, such as health care and law enforcement. It is also thought likely that interest in foreign-language learning will further diminish, and this is felt to be an unfortunate development at a time when the climate in international business competitiveness and political

136

diplomacy is one where foreign-language ability is increasingly seen as advantageous (see p. 18).

- *Educational issues* Several other kinds of argument are used in the debate – in particular, to do with educational theory and practice. For example, the pro-official position is concerned that many students in bilingual education programmes are being taught by teachers whose own level of English is of a low quality, thus inculcating an inadequate command of the language, and a 'ghetto dialect' that will mark the speakers as socially inferior. They point to the shortage of adequately trained teachers, and to the many problems in assigning students to the right kind of programme for the right length of time, and claim that bilingual programmes are not as efficient as English-immersion programmes in fostering the transition to mainstream English classes. Anti-official supporters stress the value of bilingualism as part of a child's learning experience, observing that immigrant children are more likely to do well in learning a second language if their own language is valued by the society in which they find themselves. They stress the potential for success of bilingual education programmes, arguing that the best predictor of achievement in English for immigrant children by age eighteen is the amount of time spent in bilingual classrooms. If there are inadequacies in the educational system, it is suggested, these are due to the failure of government to provide enough financial support for learning resources, educational facilities, and teacher training, and to the fact that bilingual programmes are available to only about 25 per cent of students with limited English proficiency. The 'official English' bill, it is pointed out, does virtually nothing to enable fluency in English to be universally achieved – other than simply stating that it must be. To evaluate the arguments on both sides would require a detailed consideration of such matters as teaching methods, research procedures, and assessment goals, and is too complex an area to be given summary treatment in the present book.[6] But it is

---

[6] The relationship between bilingualism and education is well addressed in Baker and Prys Jones (1998); see especially pp. 290–1 in relation to official English movements.

important to appreciate that a great deal of time has been, and continues to be, devoted to this issue.

Many of those who support the pro-official position feel that the pendulum has swung too far in the wrong direction. From a position where transitional programmes were being devised to get children into the English-speaking mainstream as quickly as possible, they now see a position where these programmes are being used to preserve cultural identity and to reduce integration. From a position where immigrants were expected to learn English, they note cases of non-immigrants in schools now having to learn the immigrant language. From a position where English was the language an immigrant needed for a job, they now note cases where a monolingual English person would have to learn an immigrant language in order to be eligible for a job. They fear a society in which people will be appointed first for linguistic reasons, and only secondly for their other abilities and experience. These fears are by no means unique to the USA, of course. They surface wherever a bilingual policy is in operation. But they are expressed with special strength in the USA, partly because of the large numbers involved, and partly because the democratic tradition is so strongly supportive of the rights of the individual.

Many anti-official supporters, unconvinced by the pro-official arguments, find that there is no alternative but to conclude that the 'official English' position is one of (consciously or unconsciously held) elitism or discrimination. Minority languages are not being protected, in their view, but restricted. An 'official English' law, according to an alternative proposal which was formulated (the 'English Plus Resolution', introduced in the House in July 1995 by Representative Jose Serrano), would be 'an unwarranted Federal regulation of self-expression' and would 'abrogate constitutional rights to freedom of expression and equal protection of the laws'. It would also 'contradict the spirit of the 1923 Supreme Court case Meyer v. Nebraska, wherein the Court declared that "The protection of the Constitution extends to all; to those who speak other languages as well as to those born with English on the tongue".' To disregard this tradition of thinking, it was argued, could make a difficult social situation still more difficult. The Serrano bill claimed that official English legislation would 'violate traditions of cultural pluralism' and 'divide communities along ethnic lines'. By contrast, multilingualism could bring benefits to a community, helping to promote empathy between different ethnic groups. The leading linguistics organization of the USA, the Linguistic Society of America, in 1995 issued a statement on language rights whose final paragraph summarized the tenor of this approach:[7]

Notwithstanding the multilingual history of the United States, the role of English as our common language has never seriously been questioned. Research has shown that newcomers to America continue to learn English at rates comparable to previous generations of immigrants. All levels of government should adequately fund programs to teach English to any resident who desires to learn it. Nonetheless, promoting our common language need not, and should not, come at the cost of violating the rights of linguistic minorities.

The 'English Plus Resolution' began by recognizing English as 'the primary language of the United States' alongside the importance of other languages spoken by US residents, and asserted that 'these linguistic resources should be conserved and developed'. It repeatedly stressed the value of multilingualism to the US community: this would 'enhance American competitiveness in global markets', 'improve United States diplomatic efforts by fostering enhanced communication and greater understanding between nations', and 'promote greater cross-cultural understanding between different racial and ethnic groups'. It recommended that the US government should pursue policies that:

(1) encourage all residents of this country to become fully proficient in English by expanding educational opportunities;
(2) conserve and develop the Nation's linguistic resources by encouraging all residents of this country to learn or maintain skills in a language other than English;
(3) assist native Americans, Native Alaskans, Native Hawaiians, and other peoples indigenous to the United States, in their efforts to prevent the extinction of their languages and cultures;

[7] Linguistic Society of America (1996).

(4) continue to provide services in languages other than English as needed to facilitate access to essential functions of government, promote public health and safety, ensure due process, promote equal educational opportunity, and protect fundamental rights, and

(5) recognize the importance of multilingualism to vital American interests and individual rights, and oppose 'English-only' measures and similar language restrictionist measures.

However, the Serrano bill made no further progress in 1996, with political attention eventually focusing exclusively on the Emerson proposal (p. 130).

By the end of 1996, the future direction of the 'official English' debate was still unsettled. The language arguments had become increasingly polarized, and forced into line with the party politics of an election year; and the emotional level of the debate had escalated. There seems to be something about the intimate relationship between language, thought, individuality, and social identity which generates strong emotions. And in a climate where supporters of official English (no matter how moderate) came to be routinely labelled 'racist', and immigrants wishing to use their own language (no matter how cultured) were castigated by such names as 'welfare hogs', it was difficult to see the grounds for compromise. The argument has continued unabated into the new millennium. The number of states enacting official English legislation increased from twenty-two in 1995 to twenty-seven in 2002, and a further round of legislation began in May 2001, when an English Language Unity Act was introduced in the House of Representatives (HR 1984). Opposition from the academic linguistic community continues to be intense.

New Englishes

Salman Rushdie comments, in an essay called 'Commonwealth literature does not exist',[8] that 'the English language ceased to be the sole possession of the English some time ago'. Indeed, when even the largest English-speaking nation, the USA, turns out to

[8] Rushdie (1991).

have only about 20 per cent of the world's English speakers (as we saw in chapter 2), it is plain that no one can now claim sole ownership. This is probably the best way of defining a genuinely global language, in fact: that its usage is not restricted by countries or (as in the case of some artificial languages) by governing bodies.

The loss of ownership is of course uncomfortable to those, especially in Britain, who feel that the language is theirs by historical right; but they have no alternative. There is no way in which any kind of regional social movement, such as the purist societies which try to prevent language change or restore a past period of imagined linguistic excellence, can influence the global outcome. In the end, it comes down to population growth. In the list of English-speaking territories shown in chapter 2, the number of first-language (L1) speakers in the inner-circle countries is currently about the same as the number of second-language (L2) English speakers in the outer-circle countries – some 400 million. But as we have seen (p. 69), the countries of the outer circle have, combined, a much greater growth rate than those of the inner circle: in 2002, an average of 2.4 per cent compared with 0.88 per cent. So, if current population and learning trends continue, the balance of speakers will change dramatically. There are probably already more L2 speakers than L1 speakers. Within fifty years, there could be up to 50 per cent more. By that time, the only possible concept of ownership will be a global one.

The remarkable number of speakers involved needs to be appreciated. In India, for example, the population has doubled since 1960, and passed a thousand million in 1999. It is thus the second most populous country in the world, after China, but its population growth rate is larger than China's (1.7 per cent in the late 1990s, as opposed to 1.1 per cent). Even at the lower estimate reported on p. 46, there are now almost as many speakers of English in India as there are in England; at the higher estimate, there are six times as many. If current English-language learning trends continue (and with satellite television and other sources of English increasingly available, it looks as if they will), this differential will continue to widen.

An inevitable consequence of these developments is that the language will become open to the winds of linguistic change in totally unpredictable ways. The spread of English around the world has already demonstrated this, in the emergence of new varieties of English in the different territories where the language has taken root. The change has become a major talking point only since the 1960s, hence the term by which these varieties are often known: 'new Englishes'. The different dialects of British and American English provide the most familiar example. These two varieties diverged almost as soon as the first settlers arrived in America.[9] By the time Noah Webster was writing his dictionaries, there were hundreds of words which were known in the USA but not in Britain, pronunciation had begun to diverge quite markedly, and spellings were in the process of change. Today, there are thousands of differences between British and American English – two countries, as George Bernard Shaw once put it, 'divided by a common language'.[10]

In the USA, a concern to develop a distinctive 'American standard' was prominent in Webster's thinking. He presented the case strongly in his *Dissertations on the English language*.[11] It was partly a matter of honour 'as an independent nation . . . to have a system of our own, in language as well as government'. It was partly a matter of common sense, because in England 'the taste of her writers is already corrupted, and her language on the decline'. And it was partly a matter of practicality, England being at 'too great a distance to be our model'. This national or 'federal' language was inevitable, Webster thought, because the exploration of the new continent would bring many new words into the language, which Britain would not share; but it also needed fostering. Spelling reform, he concluded, would be a major step in that direction: 'a difference between the English orthography and the American . . . is an object of vast political consequence'. He was right. Language and political issues are always very closely connected, as we have seen in earlier chapters.

[9] Examples are given in the section on vocabulary below, p. 158.
[10] Attributed to him in *Reader's Digest* (November 1942); virtually identical sentiments were expressed by Oscar Wilde and Dylan Thomas.
[11] Webster (1789: 22).

The forces which shaped the development of American English are many and various. They have been well summarized by US dialectologist Frederic G. Cassidy:[12]

The effect of the Revolution and of national independence was tremendous. No less a figure than Noah Webster saw here a great opportunity to cast off the 'corrupt' language of England and to rationalize and refine the language for the new nation. The attempt to found an academy for such a purpose, which had several times failed in Britain, was made once again under the leadership of Thomas Jefferson. But other forces were at work – popular forces – which were to have a powerful effect, especially when actual democracy, rather than limited upper-class governance, came to the fore under Andrew Jackson.

The surge of population westward, the phenomenon of the expanding frontier in which the restraints and standards of more settled society were thrown off, was reflected in the language. With little or no education, having to cope as best they could with harsh physical conditions, the 'conquerors of the West' became freely innovative in their language, ebullient with descriptive and metaphorical inventions – with 'tall talk', exaggerated humor, vigor that had no time for refinement.

In the East, in the cities, however, education flourished; the leading class had it and it became a national ideal: the mark of progress in any settlement was that a school had been started. Self-education, especially for talented people of humble beginnings, was widely practiced and admired. Public address, often learned in the 'school of hard knocks', carried to the people educational ideals and their kudos. Some of the interesting neologisms were the direct offspring of ignorance pretending to be learned. A whole school of humor portrayed its characters as unschooled but practically wise.

Cassidy is here thinking of the humour of such authors as Josh Billings, Artemus Ward, and other 'cracker-barrel philosophers' who delighted audiences and readers all over the USA in the late nineteenth century. 'Humin natur', comments Billings, in his homespun spelling, 'is the same all over the world, cept in Nu England, and thar its akordin tu sarcumstances.'[13]

---

[12] Cassidy (1982: 204–5).
[13] A range of illustrations from both authors are to be found in Crystal (1995a: 84).

This kind of humorous writing cannot work unless people can see it is a joke – in other words, they must be able to recognize the spellings as non-standard, and be able to identify dialect grammar and vocabulary. Webster was sixty when Billings was born. Evidently, in quite a short time, American English had settled down in its new identity, and despite its dialect differences was capable of providing a unified, literary standard which the new nation was able to recognize and to which it could respond.

Many distinctive forms also identify the Englishes of the other countries of the inner circle (p. 60): Australian English, New Zealand English, Canadian English, South African English, Caribbean English, and, within Britain, Irish, Scots, and Welsh English. Among the countries of the outer circle, several varieties have also grown in distinctiveness in recent decades, as we have seen in chapter 2. There is one group in India, Pakistan, Bangladesh, and Sri Lanka, often collectively called South Asian English. There is another group in the former British colonies in West Africa, and a further group in the former British colonies in East Africa. Other emerging varieties have been noted in the Caribbean and in parts of south-east Asia, such as Singapore.

These new Englishes are somewhat like the dialects we all recognize within our own country, except that they are on an international scale, applying to whole countries or regions. Instead of affecting mere thousands of speakers, as is typically the case with rural or urban regional dialects, they apply to millions. They are an inevitable consequence of the spread of English on a world scale. The study of language history shows that if two social groups come to be separated only by a mountain range or a wide river, they will soon begin to develop different habits of speech. It should not be surprising, then, to find new national dialects emerging when groups become separated by thousands of miles, and encounter totally different climates, fauna, and flora.

Dialects emerge because they give identity to the groups which own them. If you wish to tell everyone which part of a country you are from, you can wave a flag, wear a label on your coat, or (the most convenient solution, because it is always with you, even in the dark and around corners) speak with a distinctive accent and dialect. Similarly, on the world stage, if you wish to tell everyone which country you belong to, an immediate and direct way of doing it is to speak in a distinctive way. These differences become especially noticeable in informal settings; for example, they are currently well represented in discussion groups on the Internet.

International varieties thus express national identities, and are a way of reducing the conflict between intelligibility and identity. Because a speaker from country A is using English, there is an intelligibility bond with an English speaker of country B – and this is reinforced by the existence of a common written language. On the other hand, because speaker A is not using exactly the same way of speaking as speaker B, both parties retain their identities. It is another way of 'having your cake and eating it'.

The drive for identity was particularly dominant in the second half of the twentieth century, when the number of independent nations dramatically grew, and the membership of the United Nations more than tripled (p. 14). It is not difficult to see how so many new Englishes evolved, as a consequence. When a country becomes independent, there is a natural reaction to leave behind the linguistic character imposed by its colonial past, and to look for indigenous languages to provide a symbol of new nationhood. But in most cases this process proved unworkable. In Nigeria, for example, there were some 500 languages to choose from, each with strong ethnic roots. In such situations, the only solution was to keep using the former colonial language, which after many decades had become embedded in the fabric of local institutions. But the pressure for linguistic identity is remorseless, and it did not take long before the official adoption of English led to its adaptation. With new institutions came new ways of talking and writing; indigenous words became privileged. A locally distinctive mode of expression emerged, and in some cases began to be recorded, in the form of regional dictionary projects.[14]

[14] As early as 1967 Whitney Bolton and I were compiling a 'Dictionary of English-speaking peoples' for Cassells – a project which began by making contacts with lexicographers (or, at least, lexicographically minded linguists) working in each of the newly independent nations (as well as the long-established ones). We received initial headword-lists from several contributors, some of which already contained several thousand items. It was evident that, even within a few years of independence, people were conscious of an emerging regional lexical identity. The scale of the

Most adaptation in a New English relates to vocabulary, in the form of new words (borrowings – from several hundred language sources, in such areas as Nigeria), word-formations, word-meanings, collocations and idiomatic phrases. There are many cultural domains likely to motivate new words, as speakers find themselves adapting the language to meet fresh communicative needs. A country's biogeographical uniqueness will generate potentially large numbers of words for animals, fish, birds, insects, plants, trees, rocks, rivers and so on – as well as all the issues to do with land management and interpretation, which is an especially important feature of the lifestyle of many indigenous peoples. There will be words for foodstuffs, drinks, medicines, drugs, and the practices associated with eating, health-care, disease and death. The country's mythology and religion, and practices in astronomy and astrology, will bring forth new names for personalities, beliefs and rituals. The country's oral and perhaps also written literature will give rise to distinctive names in sagas, poems, oratory and folktales. There will be a body of local laws and customs, with their own terminology. The culture will have its technology with its own terms – such as for vehicles, house-building, weapons, clothing, ornaments and musical instruments. The whole world of leisure and the arts will have a linguistic dimension – names of dances, musical styles, games, sports – as will distinctiveness in body appearance (such as hair styles, tattoos, decoration). Virtually any aspect of social structure can generate complex naming systems – local government, family relationships, clubs and societies, and so on. Nobody has ever worked out just how much of a culture is community-specific in this way; but it must be a very significant amount. So, when a community adopts a new language, and starts to use it in relation to all areas of life, there is inevitably going to be a great deal of lexical creation.[15]

project soon became much greater than anyone had expected, and, as costs mounted, publisher enthusiasm waned. The project was cancelled after a year, leaving only the headword-lists (now long since superseded by other publications from the regional editors, such as Avis, *et al.* (1967)), a report to the publishers, and a paper to the Oxford Linguistic Circle as its epitaph.

[15] Some studies are beginning to provide semantically based classifications of new lexicon, such as Dako (2001).

The linguistic character of New Englishes

Although it has been possible to suggest answers to the question of why English has become a global language (chapters 3 and 4), the recency of the phenomenon means that we are still some distance from understanding what happens to the language when it is adopted in this way. Historical experience is no real guide to the kinds of adaptation that are currently taking place. Several of the 'New Englishes' of the past have been well studied – notably, American and Australian English – but the way the language has evolved in settings where most people are native speakers is likely to be very different from the way it will evolve in settings where most are non-native speakers. There are already signs of this happening, though it is difficult to make reliable generalizations given the social, ethnic and linguistic complexity within the countries where these developments are taking place, and the considerable variations between settings.[16] However, it is possible to identify several types of change which are taking place, and to gain a sense of their extent, from the case studies which have been carried out. This chapter focuses on grammatical and lexical issues, but does make some reference to broader patterns of interaction and to the role of nonsegmental phonology in the communication of structural meaning.

• *Grammar*

Any domain of linguistic structure and use could be the basis of variety differentiation, but the focus in comparing the traditional standards of British and American English has been almost entirely associated with vocabulary and phonology. There has been little acknowledgement of grammatical variation in those reference works which incorporate an international perspective: one grammar, talking about the distinction between British and American English, comments that 'grammatical differences are few ... lexical examples are far more numerous', and it makes only

[16] As the illustrations in Burchfield (1994) demonstrate. See also Bauer's reservations about Maori English (1994: 415) and Kachru's on South Asian English (1994: 518).

sporadic reference to possibilities in other regions.[17] The point is apparently reinforced in another, which concludes that 'grammatical differences across registers are more extensive than across dialects' and that 'core grammatical features are relatively uniform across dialects'.[18] Undoubtedly there is an impression of relative 'sameness', with very few points of absolute differentiation (e.g. AmE *gotten*), but it may well be that this is due to a set of factors which will not always obtain.

Two points are relevant. First, grammars – especially those motivated by teaching considerations – have traditionally focused on standard English, and thus essentially on printed English, which provides the foundation of that standard.[19] Non-standard varieties are mentioned only in passing. However, we know from intranational dialectology that it is here where grammatical distinctiveness is most likely to be found. New Englishes, which like intranational dialects are very much bound up with issues of local identity, are likely to display a similar direction of development. Second, because new varieties are chiefly associated with speech, rather than writing, they have also attracted less attention. Even in the major European reference grammars, which have always acknowledged the importance of the spoken language, there has nonetheless been a concentration on writing. Corpora are still massively biased towards the written language: the 100-million-word British National Corpus, for example, had at the outset only 10 per cent of its material devoted to speech. The Bank of English had a remarkable 20 million words of transcribed natural speech at the point when its corpus had reached 320 million words, but this is still only 6 per cent. The 40-million-word corpus used for the Biber *et al.* grammar (see above) is a significant improvement in proportions, with 6.4 million words of conversational speech and 5.7 million of non-conversational speech; but even 30 per cent of a corpus is an inversion of the realities of daily language use around the world.[20]

[17] Quirk, Greenbaum, Leech and Svartvik (1985: 19–20).
[18] Biber, Johansson, Leech, Conrad and Finegan (1999: 20–1).
[19] Quirk (1962: 95).
[20] For further illustration of the categories of these corpora, see Crystal (1995a: 438–41).

Traditionally, the national and international use of English has been in the hands of people who are not just literate, but for whom literacy is a significant part of their professional identity. 'Educated usage' (which usually meant 'well-educated usage'[21]) has been a long-standing criterion of what counts as English. The influence of the grammar of the written language has thus been pervasive, fuelled by a strongly prescriptive tradition in schools and an adult reliance on usage manuals which privileged writing above speech. Grammars totally devoted to speech are rare, and self-avowedly exploratory.[22] But as English becomes increasingly global, we must expect far more attention to be paid to speech. Although there is no suggestion anywhere that standard written English will diminish in importance, and literacy remains a dominant target, there is increasing evidence (reviewed below) of new spoken varieties growing up which are only partly related to the written tradition and which may even be totally independent of it. It is unlikely that any regional trends identified in a predominantly written corpus tradition will be predictive of the grammatical changes which will take place in global spoken English. Accordingly, the current view, that there is little macro-regional grammatical differentiation, may not be applicable for much longer.

But even in the available literature, with its bias towards writing, there are more signs of grammatical differentiation than the general statements suggest. This is most in evidence in the grammar by Biber *et al.*, where the results of statistical register-based comparisons are presented, and special attention is paid to areas of interaction between lexicon and grammar, with particular reference to standard British English (BrE) and American English (AmE). The view that 'core grammatical features are relatively uniform across dialects' is broadly justified, but how we interpret this depends on exactly what is meant by 'core', and just how much tolerance we allow in under the heading of 'relatively'. Certainly, when we examine colligations (i.e. lexical collocations in specific grammatical contexts) we find a multiplicity of differences. The index to Biber *et al.* identifies some sixty locations

---

[21] Quirk (1960).   [22] As with Brazil (1995).

Table 3 *(a) Some differences in British and American adverbial usage, after Biber et al. (1999).*[a]

Adverbials	Register	Example	Used in BrE	Used in AmE	Page
yesterday	newspaper	X happened yesterday	much higher		795
days of week	newspaper	X happened Wednesday		much higher	795
may be, kind of, like	conversation	I kind of knew		much higher	867
sort of	conversation	I sort of knew	much higher		867
so as linking adverbial	conversation	so, I'm hoping he'll go		higher	886
then as linking adverbial	conversation	we'll use yours, then	higher		886
adjective as adverb	conversation	make sure it runs smooth		higher	542
good as adverb	conversation	it worked out good		much higher	543
real + adjectives	conversation	that was real nice		much higher	543

[a] The table should be read as follows (from line 1): the frequency of use of the adverbial *yesterday* in newspaper English, as in 'X happened yesterday', is much higher in British English than in American English (according to the criteria of Biber *et al.*); the point is reported on p. 795 of their book.

(b) Specific adverb+adjective pairs showing differences in conversational usage, after Biber et al. (1999: 545).

Occurrence	BrE	AmE
100 + per million	very good very nice	pretty good really good
50 + per million	quite good really good	too bad very good
20 + per million	pretty good quite nice too bad fair enough	real good real quick really bad too big very nice

150

where its approach established some sort of contrastivity, and at many of these there is considerable lexico-grammatical variation. An example of this variation is given in Table 3(a), where some of the adverbial differences are noted; Table 3(b) takes the topic of adverbs modifying adjectives, and extracts the relevant differences for conversation. This kind of variation is found at several places within the grammar. For example, older semi-modals (e.g. *have to, be going to*) are noted to be 'considerably more common' in AmE, whereas recent semi-modals (e.g. *had better, have got to*) are 'more common by far' in BrE.[23] Variations are also noted with respect to aspect, modals, negation, concord, pronouns, complementation and several other areas. Although each point is relatively small in scope, the potential cumulative effect of a large number of local differences, especially of a colligational type, can be considerable. It is this which probably accounts for the impression of Britishness or Americanness which a text frequently conveys, without it being possible to find any obviously distinctive grammatical or lexical feature within it.

But whatever the grammatical differences between standard American and British English, these are likely to be small compared with the kinds of difference which are already beginning to be identified in the more recently recognized New Englishes. And areas which we might legitimately consider to be 'core' are being implicated. Several examples have been identified in case studies of particular regional varieties, as will be illustrated below; but it is important to note the limitations of these studies. The state of the art is such that the examples collected can only be illustrative of possible trends in the formation of new regional grammatical identities. There have been few attempts to adopt a more general perspective, to determine whether a feature noticed in one variety is also to be found in others, either nearby or further afield.[24] Nor do the case studies adopt the same kind of intra-regional variationist perspective as illustrated by Biber *et al.*

[23] Biber *et al.* (1999: 488–9).
[24] This point is discussed in Crystal (1995a: 358ff.). An exception is Ahulu (1995a), comparing usage in West Africa and India, and his two-part study of lexical and grammatical variation in international English, as found in postcolonial countries (1998a, 1998b).

(1999), or examine lexico-grammatical interaction. The studies are often impressionistic – careful collections of examples by linguistically trained observers, but lacking the generalizing power which only systematic surveys of usage can provide. On the other hand, during the 1990s there has been a steady growth in the use of corpora and elicitation testing.[25]

The absence of statistical data, in the literature referred to below, means that the varietal status of features identified as non-standard (with reference to British or American English) is always open to question. There are so many possibilities: a variant may be common as a localized standard form, in both written and spoken contexts, or restricted to one of these mediums; it may be formal or informal, or register-bound, occurring only in newspapers, student slang,[26] or other restricted settings; it may be idiosyncratic, as in the case of some literary creations; it may co-exist with a variant from British or American English; and it may be locally stigmatized, or even considered to be an error (by local people). Given that it has taken forty years for corpus studies of the main varieties of English to reach the stage of comparative register-specific analysis (as in Biber *et al.*), it is not surprising that relatively little such work has taken place elsewhere. But this does not mean that a compilation of sources, such as those listed in Table 4, is of no value. On the contrary, such studies are an excellent means of focusing attention on areas of potential significance within a variety, and are an invaluable source of hypotheses.

Table 4 illustrates a range of features which have already been noted, some of which are very close to what anyone might reasonably want to call 'core'. A table of this kind needs very careful interpretation. Its only purpose is to illustrate the kinds of grammatical feature being proposed as distinctive in studies of New Englishes, and it makes no claim to exhaustiveness or representativeness. Providing an example from, say, Ghana, to instantiate a feature, is not to suggest that this feature is restricted to Ghana: Ghana is simply one of the countries in which this feature may be found (as claimed by at least one of the authors identified at the right of the table), and doubtless several others also display

---

[25] As in Mesthrie (1992a), Skandera (1999). [26] Longe (1999).

Table 4 *Some potentially distinctive grammatical features of New Englishes*

Construction	Illustration	Sample sources
Sentence functions		
Rhetorical questions	Where young! (= I'm certainly not young)	Mesthrie (1993b)
	Where he'll do it! (= He certainly won't do it!)	Mesthrie (1993b)
	What I must go! (= I don't want to go)	Mesthrie (1993b)
Tag questions	He can play golf, or not?	Baskaran (1994)
	He can play golf, yes or not?	Baskaran (1994)
	You stay here first, can or not?	Baskaran (1994)
	You didn't see him, is it?	Tripathi (1990)
	He left, isn't? (= He left, didn't he?)	Mesthrie (1993b)
	You are coming to the meeting, isn't it?	Kachru (1994)
Clause elements		
SV order	at no stage it was demanded...	Baumgardner (1990)
	Why a step-motherly treatment is being...	Baumgardner (1990)
	What they are talking about?	Baskaran (1994)
	When you would like to go?	Kachru (1994)
	She is crying why?	Baskaran (1994)
Complementation	busy to create (= busy creating)	Baumgardner (1990)
	banning Americans to enter	Baumgardner (1990)
	decision for changing	Baumgardner (1990)
Object deletion	Those who cannot afford	Fisher (2000)
Adverbial position	You must finish today all your practicals	Baskaran (1994)
	Sushila is extremely a lazy girl	Baskaran (1994)
	Seldom she was at home	Baskaran (1994)
	Hardly they were seen in the library	Baskaran (1994)

(*cont.*)

Table 4 (*cont.*)

Construction	Illustration	Sample sources
End-placed conjunctions	She can talk English but	Mesthrie (1993b)
	I cooked rice too, I cooked roti too (= I cooked both rice and roti)	Mesthrie (1993b)
Topicalization (not necessarily emphatic)	Myself I do not know him	Tripathi (1990)
	That man he is tall	Tripathi (1990)
	My friend she was telling me	Mesthrie (1993a)
	His uncle he is the cause of all the worry	Baskaran (1994)
Verb phrase		
Auxiliary/Copula deletion	When you leaving?	Baskaran (1994)
	They two very good friends	Baskaran (1994)
Aspect/Tense	I am understanding it now	Mesthrie (1993a)
	He is having two Mercs	Baskaran (1994)
	I finish eat (= I have eaten)	Mesthrie (1993b)
	I already eat	Platt and Weber (1980)
	You never see him? (= Haven't you seen him?)	Mesthrie (1993b)
	waited-waited (= waited for a long time)	Mesthrie (1993b)
	to give crying crying (= always crying)	Kachru (1994)
	I have been signing yesterday	Baskaran (1994)
	I would be singing next week (expressing distant future, vs. *will*)	Baskaran (1994)
	The government shall be responsible	Fisher (2000)
Phrasal verbs	cope up with [something]	Tripathi (1990)
	stress on [something]	Baumgardner (1990)
	fill this form	Skandera (1999)
	pick the visitor (= pick up)	Fisher (2000)
	participate a seminar	Baumgardner (1990)
	pluck courage	Fisher (2000)

Table 4 (*cont.*)

Construction	Illustration	Sample sources
Noun phrase		
Preposed elements	milk bottle (= a bottle of milk)	Baumgardner (1990)
	knife bread (= bread knife)	Tripathi (1990)
	under construction bridge (= bridge which is under construction)	Baumgardner (1990)
	detrimental to health medicines	Baumgardner (1990)
Apposition	Johnny uncle (= uncle Johnny)	Mesthrie (1993b)
	Naicker teacher (= teacher, Mr Naicker)	Mesthrie (1993b)
Number	aircrafts, equipments, luggages, machineries, stationeries, damages (= damage), jewelleries, cutleries, furnitures	Ahulu (1998b)
	trouser	Awonusi (1990)
Article use	a good advice	Ahulu (1998b)
	a luggage	Ahulu (1998b)
	There'll be traffic jam	Baskaran (1994)
	She was given last chance	Baskaran (1994)
Pronoun deletion	Did you find? (something previously mentioned)	Mesthrie (1993a)
	If you take, you must pay	Baskaran (1994)
Other constructions		
Prepositions	request for	Gyasi (1991)
	investigate into	Gyasi (1991)
	gone to abroad	Gyasi (1991)
	ask from him	Awonusi (1990)
	discuss about politics	Awonusi (1990)
	return back	Tripathi (1990)
Comparatives	more better	Tripathi (1990)
	younger to	Tripathi (1990)
	junior than	Tripathi (1990)
Postpositions	Durban-side (= near Durban)	Mesthrie (1993b)
	morning-part (= in the morning)	Mesthrie (1993b)
	twelve-o-clock-time (= at twelve o'clock)	Mesthrie (1993b)

(*cont.*)

Table 4 (*cont.*)

Construction	Illustration	Sample sources
Particles	I told you, what (= Don't you remember, I told you)	Baskaran (1994)
	He is really serious, man (= I'm telling you)	Baskaran (1994)
	He's a real miser, one (= a typical miser)	Baskaran (1994)
	He's not the eldest, lah (= I'm telling you)	Baskaran (1994)
	Where you going ah?	Preshous (2001)
	We are going, oo (= right now)	Ahulu (1995b)
	He is tall, paa (He is very tall)	Ahulu (1995b)
Reduplication	now-now (= soon, at once)	Mesthrie (1993a)
	who-who (= who plural, whoever)	Mesthrie (1993b)
	what what (= whatever)	Fisher (2000)
	one-one (= one each)	Mesthrie (1993b)
	quick-quick (= very fast)	Mesthrie (1993b)
	tear-tear (= tear to shreds)	Ahulu (1995b)
	big big fish (= many fish)	Mehrotra (1997)
	good good morning (intimate tone)	Mehrotra (1997)
Lexical morphology	coloured television	Awonusi (1990)
	repairer (= repairman)	Awonusi (1990)
	second handed	Awonusi (1990)
	proudy	Tripathi (1990)
	poorness	Mesthrie (1993b)
	imprudency	Fisher (2000)
	delayance	Gyasi (1991)
	costive (= costly)	Gyasi (1991)
	matured (= mature)	Gyasi (1991)
	storeyed (= with several floors)	Fisher (2000)

it. The examples are all taken from the individual studies. No attempt is made to evaluate the standing of the author's claim, which in many cases is based on anecdotal instances observed in local newspapers, advertisements, conversation and so on. Taken together, it is the range of examples which is intriguing, leaving little doubt that the domain of grammar has to be considered as central, alongside vocabulary and phonology, in investigating the linguistic distinctiveness of New Englishes.

Examples like those given in Table 4 raise some interesting questions. It is not always clear whether a new feature arises as a result of transference from a contrasting feature in a local contact language or is a general property of English foreign-language learning, though individual studies sometimes suggest one or the other. The process of change is evidently rapid and pervasive, and origins are usually obscure. We need more diachronic typological studies.[27] But a synchronic comparison of a distinctive English construction with the corresponding construction in the contact languages of a region is usually illuminating, and well worth doing, as it is precisely this interaction that is likely to be the most formative influence on the identity of a New English. For example, Alsagoff, Bao and Wee analyse a type of *why + you* construction in Colloquial Singapore English (CSgE), illustrated by *Why you eat so much?* – a construction which signals a demand for justification (i.e. 'unless there is a good reason, you should not eat so much').[28] There are parallels in BrE and AmE: *Why eat so much?* (which would usually suggest 'I don't think you should') vs. *Why do you eat so much?* (which allows the reading 'I genuinely want to know'). The authors point out that the verb in such constructions is typically in its base form (not *-ing*) and dynamic (not stative), and thus shows similarities with the imperative, from which (they argue) the *why* construction inherits its properties. They draw attention to such constructions as *You hold on, OK*, which are somewhat impolite in BrE and AmE, but not considered offensive in CSgE; indeed, the presence of *you* is considered more polite than its absence. Thus, they conclude, *Why you eat so much?* is more polite than *Why eat so much?* They explain this reversal with reference to influence from Chinese, where the imperative allows the use of second-person pronouns to reduce any face-threatening impact.

While it is of course possible that other contact languages could have imperative constructions of a similar kind to those occurring in Chinese, and could thus influence a local variety of English in

---

[27] Of the kind illustrated by Schneider (2000).
[28] Alsagoff, Bao and Wee (1998).

the same way, the probability is that such interactions are going to be specific to the contact situation in an individual country. Especially in a multilingual country, where English is being influenced by a 'melting-pot' of other languages (such as Malay, Tamil and Chinese in Singapore), the likelihood of a particular constellation of influences being replicated elsewhere is remote. Distinctive grammatical features are also likely to be increasingly implicated in the 'mixed languages' which arise from code-switching (see further below). Moreover, as the CSgE example suggests, even features of grammar which superficially resemble those in standard BrE or AmE might turn out to be distinctive, once their pragmatic properties are taken into account. Modal verbs, for example, are likely to be particularly susceptible to variation, though the effects are not easy to identify. In short, there is every likelihood of 'core' features of English grammar becoming a major feature of the description of New Englishes, as time goes by.

- *Vocabulary*

As we have seen (p. 146), it does not take long before new words enter a language, once the language arrives in a fresh location. Borrowings from indigenous languages are especially noticeable. For example, the first permanent English settlement in North America was in Jamestown, Virginia, in 1607; and loan-words from Indian languages were introduced into contemporary writing virtually immediately. Captain John Smith, writing in 1608, describes a *racoon*; *totem* is found in 1609; *caribou* and *opossum* are mentioned in 1610.[29] However, the long-term role of borrowings, in relation to the distinctive identity of a 'New English', is unclear. In the case of American English, relatively few of the Amerindian loan-words which are recorded in the seventeenth and eighteenth centuries became a permanent part of the standard language. Mencken refers to a list of 132 Algonquian loans in which only 36 are still in standard American English, the others having become obsolete or surviving only in local dialects (e.g. *squantersquash*, *cockarouse*, *cantico*). Australia would

[29] Mencken (1945: 169).

later also demonstrate a similar paucity of indigenous words. On the other hand, the amount of borrowing from an indigenous language is extremely sensitive to sociopolitical pressures, as is evident in contemporary New Zealand, where loans from Maori are increasing.[30]

The amount of borrowing is also influenced by the number of cultures which co-exist, and the status which their languages have achieved. In a highly multilingual country, such as South Africa, Malaysia or Nigeria, where issues of identity are critical, we might expect a much greater use of loan-words. There is already evidence of this in the range of words collected in the *Dictionary of South African English*, for example.[31] In some sections of this book, depending on the initial letter-preferences of the contributing languages, there are long sequences of loan-words – *aandag*, *aandblom*, *aap*, *aar*, *aardpyp*, *aardvark*, *aardwolf*, *aas* and *aasvoël* (all from Afrikaans) are immediately followed by *abadala*, *abafazi*, *abakhaya*, *abakwetha*, *abantu*, *abaphansi*, *abathagathi* and *abelungu* (all from Nguni languages). Only on the next page of the dictionary do we encounter items from British English such as *administrator* and *advocate*. The influence of local languages is also apparent in the form of loan-translations, such as *afterclap* and *after-ox* (from Afrikaans *agter* + *klap* ('flap') and *agter* + *os*, respectively), and in hybrid forms where a foreign root is given an English affix, as in *Afrikanerdom* and *Afrikanerism*, or where two languages are involved in a blend, as in *Anglikaans*. There was already a salient loan-word presence in South African English, even before the 1994 constitution recognized eleven languages as official (including English). We might therefore expect the status of these languages to be reflected in due course by a further significant growth in the number of loan-words into South African English; but the linguistic outcome will depend on such factors as the extent to which the newfound official status of these languages is supported by economic and political realities, and the extent to which their lexical character itself changes as a result of

---

[30] For example, some 700 out of the 6,000 headwords in Orsman (1997) are of Maori origin.

[31] Branford and Branford (1978/91).

Anglicization. Some cultural domains are likely to manifest this growth sooner than others – such as restaurant menus.[32]

All the standard processes of lexical creation are encountered when analysing the linguistic distinctiveness of New Englishes.[33] Examples of lexical morphology have already been given (see Table 4). Several studies of Pakistani English, for example, have shown the important role played by the various kinds of word-formation.[34] Compounding from English elements is found in such items as *wheelcup* ('hub-cap') and *side-hero* ('supporting actor'), with some elements proving to be especially productive: *-lifter* (cf. *shoplifter*) has generated many new words (e.g. *car lifter*, *luggage lifter*, *book lifter*), as has *wallah/walla* ('one who does something', e.g. *exam-centre-walla*, *coachwalla*). Hybrid compounds, using Urdu and English elements, in either order, are also notable: *khas deposit* ('special deposit'), *double roti* ('bread'). Distinctive prefixation is found, as in *anti-mullah* and *deconfirm*, and there is a wide range of distinctive suffixation, using both English and Urdu bases: compare *endeavourance*, *ruinification*, *cronydom*, *abscondee*, *wheatish*, *scapegoatism*, *oftenly*, *upliftment*, alongside *begumocracy*, *sahibism*, *sifarashee* (*sifarash* ('favour')), *babuize* (*babu* ('clerk')). Word-class conversion is illustrated by such verbs as *to aircraft*, *to slogan*, *to tantamount*, and by such noun forms as *the injureds*, *the deads*. Various processes of abbreviation, clipping and blending, are in evidence: *d/o* ('daughter of'), *r/o* ('resident of'), *admit card*, *by-polls*. Baumgardner (1998) also illustrates distinctive collocations, both English only (e.g. *discuss threadbare*, *have a soft corner*) and English/Urdu combinations (e.g. *commit zina* ('adultery'), *recite kalam* ('verse')).

Finally, we can illustrate the many examples in which a word or phrase from a well-established variety is adopted by a New English and given a new meaning or use, without undergoing any structural change. In Jamaican English, for example, we find such meaning changes as *cockpit* ('type of valley') and *beverage*

---

[32] For example, Awonusi (1990) lists *agidi, gari, eba, iyan, edikagong, suya, dodo, foofoo, moinmoin, efo elegusi* and other items found in a menu written in Nigerian English. See also the food list in Dako (2001: 40).
[33] Bauer (1983: chapter 7).   [34] Baumgardner (1993, 1998).

in the restricted sense of 'lemonade'.[35] In Ghana, we find *heavy* in the sense of 'gorgeous' and *brutal* in the sense of 'very nice', and a number of semantic shifts, including *maiden name* meaning 'given name' (applied to males) and *linguist* meaning 'spokesman for the chief'.[36] In parts of South Africa, *lounge* has come to be applied to certain types of restaurant and places of entertainment – one might see the name of an Indian restaurant such as *Bhagat's Vegetarian Lounge*, or a phrase such as *beer lounge*.[37] There are also many words which keep the same meaning, but display a different frequency of use compared with British or American English, such as the greater frequency of Jamaican *bawl* ('shout', 'weep').

Lists of lexical examples of this kind, which can be found in many sources, all suffer from similar problems. Because the investigator has focused on an individual country, it is often unclear, as in the discussion of grammar, whether a particular word is restricted to that country or whether it is also used in nearby countries. This is a special problem in South Asia and West Africa, where the linguistic identity of several adjacent countries is in question, but it is a problem which can be encountered anywhere. It is also unclear, especially in historical studies with limited source material, just how much of the lexicon proposed as regionally distinctive is in fact personally idiosyncratic – a nonce usage, perhaps, or a piece of lexical play – or no longer in use. Authors sometimes express their doubts in the description: for example, Cassidy and Le Page add, after their inclusion of *corner* meaning 'variation' (as in 'It no have no more corner', said of a song), 'perhaps an individualism'. To say that Pakistani, Indian, Nigerian and other lexical norms are emerging is probably true, but we need to be very careful about the items used to substantiate such claims.

When local vocabulary from all sources is collected, a regional dictionary can quickly grow to several thousand items. There are over 3,000 items recorded in the first edition of the *Dictionary of South African English*, and later editions and collections show the

[35] Cassidy and Le Page (1967).
[36] The first examples are from Ahulu (1995b), the second ones from Dako (2001).
[37] Branford and Branford (1978/91).

number to be steadily growing (there are a further 2,500 entries already added in a 1996 edition). South African Indian English alone has 1,400. The *Dictionary of New Zealand English* has 6,000 entries. The *Concise Australian national dictionary* has 10,000. There are over 15,000 entries in the *Dictionary of Jamaican English* and 20,000 in the *Dictionary of Caribbean English usage*. Trinidad and Tobago alone produced some 8,000.[38]

It should be noted that totals of this kind tend to be of individual lexical items only. The lists may contain a fair sprinkling of idioms; but collocational distinctiveness is on the whole not represented. Collocations, however, are likely to prove one of the most distinctive domains of varietal differentiation. A selection of collocational variation, along with some examples of distinctive idioms, is given in Table 5.

Even in countries where the number of localized words is relatively small, their effect on the character of the local English can be great, for two reasons. The new words are likely to be frequently used within the local community, precisely because they relate to distinctive notions there. And these words tend not to occur in isolation: if a conversation is about, say, local politics, then the names of several political parties, slogans and other allusions are likely to come into the same discourse, making it increasingly impenetrable. 'Blairite MP in New Labour Sleaze Trap, say Tories' might be a British newspaper example – six words with British political meanings or overtones used in quick succession. Exactly the same kind of piling up of foreign expressions can be heard, and often read, in areas where New Englishes are emerging. In this example from the South African *Sunday Times*, all the local words are Afrikaans in origin:[39] 'It is interesting to recall that some verkrampte Nationalists, who pose now as super Afrikaners, were once bittereinder bloedsappe' (*verkramp* ('bigoted'); *bittereinder*

---

[38] These figures in this paragraph come from the following works: for South Africa, Branford and Branford (1978/91) and Silva (1996); for South African Indian English, Mesthrie (1992b); for New Zealand, Orsman (1997); for Australia, Hughes (1989); for Jamaica, Cassidy and Le Page (1967); for the Caribbean generally, Allsopp (1996); and for Trinidad and Tobago, Winer (1989). Görlach (1995) provides a lexicographic review.
[39] Branford and Branford (1978/91), under 'SAP'.

Table 5 *Some distinctive collocations and idioms noted in Pakistan, Nigeria and Ghana*

Example	Gloss (if needed)	Sample source
observe a death anniversary		Baumgardner (1990)
raise slogans against		Baumgardner (1990)
take out a procession		Baumgardner (1990)
take light	cut power supply	Awonusi (1990), Bamiro (1994)
senior sister	elder	Awonusi (1990), Bamiro (1994)
wash mouth	brush teeth	Awonusi (1990), Bamiro (1994)
next tomorrow	day after tomorrow	Awonusi (1990), Bamiro (1994)
morning meal	breakfast	Awonusi (1990), Bamiro (1994)
baby lawyer	young lawyer	Awonusi (1990), Bamiro (1994)
hear French	understand	Awonusi (1990), Bamiro (1994)
hear the smell		Gyasi (1991), Ahulu (1994, 1995b)
lorry station		Gyasi (1991), Ahulu (1994, 1995b)
chop box	box for keeping food in	Gyasi (1991), Ahulu (1994, 1995b)
Idioms		
declare a surplus	throw a party	Awonusi (1990), Bamiro (1994)
recite offhead	speak spontaneously	Awonusi (1990), Bamiro (1994)
put sand in one's gari	interfere with one's good luck	Awonusi (1990), Bamiro (1994)
take in	become pregnant	Awonusi (1990), Bamiro (1994)
give me chance/way	let me pass	Gyasi (1991), Ahulu (1994, 1995b)
I'm not financial	have no money	Gyasi (1991), Ahulu (1994, 1995b)

('die-hard of the Anglo-Boer war'); *bloedsappe* ('staunch member of the United Party')).

- ## *Code-switching*

With illustrations like the one from the *Sunday Times*, it is not difficult to see how the process of variety differentiation might develop further. It was not just an Afrikaans noun which was distinctive, in the above example; it was an adjective + noun combination. The door is therefore open to make use of strings larger than a phrase. Even in British English, there are instances of clause- or sentence-size chunks being borrowed from a foreign language (*Je ne sais quoi, c'est la vie*), so in situations where contact with other languages is routine and socially pervasive, we would expect this process to appear on a large scale, and eventually to have a dramatic impact on the character of the language, in the form of code-switching, the process in which people rely simultaneously on two or more languages to communicate with each other.

The increase in code-switching is evidently one of the most noticeable features of the situations in which New Englishes are emerging. Any loan-word could be viewed as a minimalist example of code-switching, but the notion is more persuasive when it is found in stretches of utterance which can be given a syntactic definition. McArthur gives an example of a leaflet issued by the HongkongBank in 1994 for Filipino workers in Hong Kong who send money home to their families.[40] It is a bilingual leaflet, in English and Tagalog, but in the Tagalog section a great deal of English is mixed in. Here is a short extract: 'Mag-deposito ng pera mula sa ibang HongkongBank account, at any Hongkongbank ATM, using your Cash Card. Mag-transfer ng regular amount bawa't buwan (by Standing Instruction) galang sa inyong Current o Savings Account, whether the account is with Hongkong Bank or not.' This kind of language is often described using a compound name – in this case, Taglish (for Tagalog-English). It is unclear whether this kind of mixing is idiosyncratic to a particular institution, genre or region; but it illustrates the extent to

---

[40] McArthur (1998: 13).

which it is possible to go, and still retain an identity which is at least partly English. Whether one should call it a variety of English or something else is not yet clear.[41]

Mixed varieties involving English are now found everywhere, with colourful nicknames attached – Franglais, Tex-Mex, Chinglish, Japlish, Singlish, Spanglish, Denglish or Angleutsch, and many more. These terms are now widely used regardless of the direction of the mixing: they have been applied to a variety of a language which has been much anglicized as well as to a variety of English which has made use of other languages. Whether the direction makes a difference to the type of language used is uncertain. What is important to note is that general attitudes towards these phenomena are slowly changing (though still receiving much establishment opposition – see below). Formerly, such names were only ever used as scornful appellations by the general public. People would sneer at Tex-Mex, and say it was neither one language nor the other, or refer to it as 'gutter-speak' used by people who had not learned to talk properly. But we can hardly call a variety like Taglish gutter-speak when it is being used in writing by a major banking corporation. And when these 'mixed' languages are analysed, it is found that they are full of great complexity and subtlety of expression – as we would expect, if people have the resources of two languages to draw upon, rather than one.

McArthur's aim was to draw attention to the remarkable 'messiness' which characterizes the current world English situation, especially in second-language contexts. Typically, a New English is not a homogeneous entity, with clear-cut boundaries, and an easily definable phonology, grammar and lexicon. On the contrary, communities which are putting English to use are doing so in several different ways. As McArthur puts it, 'stability and flux go side by side, centripetal and centrifugal forces operating at one and the same time'.[42] And when actual examples of language in use are analysed, in such multilingual settings as Malaysia and Singapore, all kinds of unusual hybrids come to light. Different

---

[41] See the discussion in Görlach (1996: 162).
[42] McArthur (1998: 2).

degrees of language mixing are apparent: at one extreme, a sentence might be used which is indistinguishable from standard English; at the other, a sentence might use so many words and constructions from a contact language that it becomes unintelligible to those outside a particular community. In between, there are varying degrees of hybridization, ranging from the use of a single lexical borrowing within a sentence to several borrowings, and from the addition of a single borrowed syntactic construction (such as a tag question) to a reworking of an entire sentence structure. In addition, of course, the pronunciation shows similar degrees of variation, from a standard British or American accent to an accent which diverges widely from such standards both in segmental and nonsegmental (intonational, rhythmical) ways.[43]

It is possible to see this within a few lines of conversation, as in this example from Malaysia ('Malenglish'), in which two Kuala Lumpur women lawyers are talking.[44] The first speaker is a Tamil; the second is Chinese; and both have learned English and Malay as additional languages.

CHANDRA: Lee Lian, you were saying you wanted to go shopping, nak pergi tak?
LEE LIAN: Okay, okay, at about twelve, can or not?
CHANDRA: Can lah, no problem one! My case going to be adjourned anyway.
LEE LIAN: What you looking for? Furnitures or kitchenwares? You were saying, that day, you wanted to beli some barang-barang for your new house.
CHANDRA: Yes lah! Might as well go window-shopping a bit at least. No chance to ronda otherwise. My husband, he got no patience one!
LEE LIAN: You mean you actually think husbands got all that patience ah? No chance man! Yes or not?
CHANDRA: Betul juga. No chance at all! But if anything to do with their stuff – golf or snooker or whatever, then dia pun boleh sabar one.

---

[43] See below, and also Crystal (1996), Goh (1998).
[44] Baskaran (1994).

LEE LIAN: Yes lah, what to do? It still is a man's world, in that sense! Anyway, we better go now – so late already – wait traffic jam, then real susah!

We can reorganize the data in this extract to show the hybridization. At the top is a sentence which could be called Standard Colloquial English; below it are other sentences which show increasing degrees of departure from this norm, grammatically and lexically. At the bottom is a sentence which is entirely Colloquial Malay.

Standard English
Might as well go window-shopping a bit at least.
It still is a man's world, in that sense!
Increasing grammatical hybridization
My case going to be adjourned anyway. [auxiliary verb omitted]
wait traffic jam [preposition and article omitted]
Can lah, no problem one! ['I can'; *lah* and *one* are emphatic particles]
Okay, okay, at about twelve, can or not? [distinctive tag question in English]
you were saying you wanted to go shopping, nak pergi tak? [tag question in Malay 'Want to go, not?']
Increasing lexical hybridization
No chance to ronda otherwise. [Malay 'loaf']
then real susah! [Malay 'difficult']
You were saying, that day, you wanted to beli some barang-barang. [Malay 'buy...things']
But if anything to do with their stuff – golf or snooker or whatever, then dia pun boleh sabar one. [Malay 'he too can be patient']
Malay
Betul juga. ['True also']

Continua of this kind have long been recognized in creole language studies. What is novel, as McArthur points out, is the way phenomena of this kind have become so widespread, happening simultaneously in communities all over the world. After reviewing several speech situations, he concludes: 'Worldwide communication centres on Standard English, which however radiates out into many kinds of English and many other languages, producing

clarity here, confusion there, and novelties and nonsenses everywhere. The result can be – often is – chaotic, but despite the
blurred edges, this latter-day Babel manages to work.'[45]

• *Other domains*

Grammar and vocabulary are not the only domains within which
linguistic distinctiveness manifests itself among the New Englishes
of the world: pragmatic and discoursal domains also need to be
taken into account. However, studies in these areas are few, anecdotal and programmatic. The Singaporean case described above
is somewhat exceptional in its depth of detail. The sources listed
in Table 4 give only sporadic examples, such as the nomenclature
of titles, kinship terms and politeness strategies. In the Nigerian
sources, for example, occupation titles are reported to cover a
wider range of cases than in British English (e.g. *Engineer X*) and
to allow different combinations (e.g. *Dr Mrs X, Alhaja Engineer
Chief X*). In the Zambian and Ghanaian studies, terms such as
father, *mother*, *brother*, *sister* and so on are shown to have different ranges of application, reflecting the internal structure of
the family (e.g. the name *father* can be given to more than one
person). Also in Ghana, and doubtless often elsewhere, reference
is made to a distinctive strategy in which someone says *sorry* to
express sympathy when something unfortunate happens to someone else, even when the speaker is not at fault. These are isolated
observations. As yet there is nothing even approximating to a
systematic description of the pragmatics of world English.

There is more to be said with reference to phonology. Most
of the descriptive reports in Table 4 do give some account of the
vowel and consonant segments characteristic of a variety. However, few give details of the non-segmental characteristics of New
Englishes, especially of the general character of their intonation
and rhythm, and of the way in which these factors interact with
vowels and consonants.[46] The general lack of attention to the

[45] McArthur (1998: 22).
[46] For non-segmental phonology, in its sense of the whole range of prosodic
and paralinguistic features of a language, see Crystal (1969). Jowitt (2000)

domain is regrettable, as there is plainly a major factor in evidence here which has a potentially significant structural impact, especially in the way in which it affects the comprehension of spoken English. One author comments:[47] 'Most Nigerian languages are "syllable-timed" languages . . . However close a Nigerian speaker approximates to consonant and vowel qualities, if he uses "syllable-timing" when speaking English, he may well be faced by total incomprehension on the part of any listener who is a native speaker of English.' The distinction between syllable-timing (found, for example, in French, Greek, Italian, Spanish, Hindi, Yoruba, Telugu, Indonesian and the majority of the world's languages) and stress-timing (found for example in English, Russian, Arabic, Portuguese, Swedish, Thai, German, Welsh) goes back to Kenneth Pike:[48] the former term suggests that all syllables occur at regular time intervals, whether they are stressed or not; the latter that the stressed syllables fall at regular intervals, whether they are separated by unstressed syllables or not. The distinction is widely referred to in English Language Teaching manuals, notwithstanding the criticism it has received. It is now known that languages vary greatly in the amount of stress-timing or syllable-timing they employ, and that there is more to rhythmical prominence than timing: segmental sonority, syllabic weight and lexical stress are major factors in affecting auditory impressions of rhythm.[49] And even within a language, both stress-timing and syllable-timing can be heard in varying degrees. The more formal the speech, for example, the more rhythmical it is likely to be. Peter Roach concludes that 'There is no language which is totally syllable-timed or totally stress-timed – all languages display both sorts of timing . . . [and] different types of timing will be exhibited by the same speaker on different occasions and in different contexts.'[50] And Laver suggests replacing the terms by 'syllable-based' and 'stress-based' respectively, a suggestion which will be followed here.[51]

on Nigerian English is an impressive example of intonational and comparative detail.
[47] Dunstan (1969: 29–30).   [48] Pike (1945: 35).
[49] Laver (1994: 527).   [50] Roach (1982: 78).
[51] Laver (1994: 528–9).

Most people would accept Pike's judgement that English – for at least 500 years – has been essentially stress-based, with just occasional use of syllable-based speech. But the contact with other languages which is part of the context of New Englishes is fundamentally changing this situation. The vast majority of these Englishes are syllable-based, as the following observations suggest:[52]

For those Africans whose first language is syllable-timed (as many are), the resultant pronunciation of a word such as *society*...is very different from what is heard in England or America...The use of tone rather than stress, and of syllable-timing rather than stress-timing, combine to make some African English strikingly different from other varieties in pitch and rhythm...One of the most prominent features of Singaporean English is the use of syllable-timed rhythm...Rhythmically, Standard Filipino English is syllable-timed...Rhythm [in Hawaiian English] varies from the stress-timing usual in English to the syllable-timing characteristic of much Hawaiian Creole.

Type B Indian speakers [i.e. those with a rhotic accent] sometimes use patterns of accentuation that are different from the patterns in native English. The rhythm is also different from the stress-timed rhythm of native English.

SABE [South African Black English] maintains an unchanging rate of syllable utterance (tempo) over given periods of time, unlike SAE [South African English]...In this particular respect, therefore, SABE shows 'syllable-timed' characteristics.

These general impressions must be interpreted cautiously. As detailed studies emerge, descriptive generalizations will need to be refined. For example, the impression that structural words are stressed in syllable-timed speech will need some qualification, as some of these words tend to attract stress more than others. This is reported for Singaporean English, for example, where the stressing of demonstratives and modal verbs has been noted as a feature of this variety.[53] Another study reports the use of individual strategies in coping with timing in second-language English.[54] And I

---

[52] The first set of quotations is from Wells (1982: 642, 644, 646, 647, 651); the second from Bansal (1990: 227); the third from Lanham (1990: 250).
[53] Deterding (1994).   [54] Bond and Fokes (1985).

have myself described several differences in syllable-based speech extracts recorded from India, Ghana, Guyana and Jamaica.[55] Whether these differences amount to systematic regional differences is unclear. However, these variations do not remove the impression that some kind of syllable-based speech among second-language English learners is widespread, apparently affecting all areas where new varieties are emerging, in Africa, South Asia, South-East Asia and the Caribbean.

The emergence of widespread syllable-based speech in what was formerly a stress-based hegemony has repeatedly given rise to problems of comprehension, when speakers from both constituencies interact. Individual words can be misinterpreted by listeners used only to a stress-based system because of failure to identify phonological structure. Grammatical patterns can be misheard because of the unfamiliar stressing of structural words. Lexical items can be completely unrecognized. The examples in the sources above are all to do with the difficulty faced by stress-based speakers understanding syllable-based speakers. It is unclear whether there are difficulties in the opposite direction, or whether syllable-based speakers misunderstand each other any more than stress-based ones do. But there is no doubt that a problem exists when these varieties come into contact, and that it can often be severe. Moreover, as perhaps three-quarters of English speakers in the world are now speaking varieties of English which are syllable-based, a question-mark must hang over the long-term future of the stress-based system.

Is it likely that, one day, the standard English of Britain or the USA will become syllable-based? At present, the L2 varieties are not sufficiently prestigious for them to become models for first-language speakers – though some syllable-based speech has come to be part of young people's phonological repertoire, notably in the rap chanting of popular songs and in play renditions of alien, Dalek-like speech.[56] And it would take only a small number of social changes for the situation to alter – for example, the appointment to high office in first-language countries of people with strong Hispanic or African-American Creole accents. But

[55] Crystal (1996).   [56] Crystal (1995b).

at present, in most of the second-language countries, the stress-timed models are still the prestige ones, and there are signs of these being reinforced, as the increased availability of satellite television (e.g. in India) makes access to them more routine. The implications for language learning are considerable: certainly, it suggests a move away from the typical learning situation where students (whose mother-tongue is syllable-based) find themselves regularly taught by teachers (whose English is already syllable-based) with very little opportunity to hear mother-tongue stress-based speech. If this situation is now in the process of change, we may see an end to the fostering of syllable-based norms through the traditional reliance on second-language pedagogical models.

Whether in the long term stress-based speech will replace syllable-based speech, or vice versa, is impossible to say. But attention should also be paid to a third possibility – that second-language learners will become competent in both kinds of speech, continuing to use syllable-based speech for local communication, as a sign of national identity, and switching to stress-based speech for international communication, as a means of ensuring intelligibility. Multidialectism already exists in many sociolinguistic situations (see below), and it would be a natural development for it to eventually incorporate rhythmicality. Rhythm, after all, is always present in speech – and is therefore much more 'available' as a signal of identity than are individual segmental phonemes, nuclear tones, lexical items and other putative markers of style. Whatever its phonetic basis, its sociolinguistic future seems assured.

The future of English as a world language

Language is an immensely democratising institution. To have learned a language is immediately to have rights in it. You may add to it, modify it, play with it, create in it, ignore bits of it, as you will. And it is just as likely that the course of the English language is going to be influenced by those who speak it as a second or foreign language as by those who speak it as a mother-tongue. Fashions count, in language, as anywhere else. And fashions are a function of numbers. As we have seen (p. 69), the total number of mother-tongue speakers in the world is steadily falling, as a proportion of world English users. It is perfectly possible (as the example of rapping suggests) for a linguistic fashion to be started by a group of second- or foreign-language learners, or by those who speak a creole or pidgin variety, which then catches on among other speakers. And as numbers grow, and second/foreign-language speakers gain in national and international prestige, usages which were previously criticized as 'foreign' – such as a new concord rule (*three person*), variations in countability (*furnitures, kitchen-wares*) or verb use (*he be running*) – can become part of the standard educated speech of a locality, and may eventually appear in writing.

What power and prestige is associated with these new varieties of English? It is all happening so quickly that it is difficult to be sure; there have been so few studies. But impressionistically, we can see several of these new linguistic features achieving an increasingly public profile, in their respective countries. Words become used less self-consciously in the national press – no longer being put in inverted commas, for example, or given a gloss. They come to be adopted, often at first with some effort, then more naturally, by first-language speakers of English in the locality. Indeed, the canons of local political correctness, in the best sense of that phrase, may foster a local usage, giving it more prestige than it could ever have dreamed of – a good example is the contemporary popularity in New Zealand English of Maori words (and the occasional Maori grammatical feature, such as the dropping of the definite article before the people name *Maori* itself). And, above all, the local words begin to be used at the prestigious levels of society – by politicians, religious leaders, socialites, pop musicians and others. Using local words is then no longer to be seen as slovenly or ignorant, within a country; it is respectable; it may even be 'cool'.

The next step is the move from national to international levels. These people who are important in their own communities – whether politicians or pop stars – start travelling abroad. The rest of the world looks up to them, either because it wants what they have, or because it wants to sell them something. And the result is the typical present-day scenario – an international gathering (political, educational, economic, artistic . . .) during which senior visitors use, deliberately or unselfconsciously, a word or phrase from their own country which would not be found in the traditional standards of British or American English. Once upon a time, the reaction would have been to condemn the usage as ignorance. Today, it is becoming increasingly difficult to say this, or even to think it, if the visitors have more degrees than the visited, or own a bigger company, or are social equals in every way. In such circumstances, one has to learn to live with the new usage, as a feature of increasing diversity in English. It can take a generation or two, but it does happen. It happened within fifty years between Britain and America: by 1842, Charles Dickens was making observations about American linguistic usage – expressing amazement, for example, at the many ways that Americans use the verb *fix* – in tones of delight, not dismay.[57] But, whatever your attitude towards new usages – and there will always be people who sneer at diversity – there is no getting away from the fact that, these days, regional national varieties of English are increasingly being used with prestige on the international scene.

If these New Englishes are becoming standardized, as markers of educated regional identity, what is taking their place elsewhere within the social spectrum of these communities? Here, very little descriptive research has been done, but there are enough anecdotal reports to suggest the way things are going. When actual examples of language in use are analysed, in such multilingual settings as Malaysia and Singapore, we immediately encounter varieties which make use of the different levels of code-mixing illustrated above. Conversations of that kind, between well-educated people, are now heard at grass-roots level in communities all over the English-speaking world.[58] However, establishment attitudes towards these varieties are still generally negative. In 1999, for example, Prime Minister Goh Chok Tong of Singapore devoted several minutes of his National Day Rally speech to a plea for Singaporeans to cut down on their use of Singlish (a hybrid of English, Chinese and Malay) and to maintain the use of Standard English, if the country's aims for a greater international role

---

[57] In his *American Notes*, revised in 1868. The example is taken from chapter 9.

[58] For example, Mesthrie (1992a), Siegel (1995).

were to be realized. He illustrated this part of the speech with some Singlish expressions, then focused his anxiety on the influence of the media, and in particular the leading character from the country's highly popular television sitcom, Phua Chu Kang ('PCK'), known for his rapid, fluent Singlish. The prime minister then approached the Television Corporation of Singapore, and asked them to do something about it; they then agreed to enrol PCK in some basic English classes so that he could improve his Standard English. The action was widely reported both within the country and abroad, and not without scepticism; as the British *Independent* put it, the chastising of Phua Chu Kang 'was something like the Queen rebuking Del Boy during the opening of parliament'.[59]

That language should receive such a high profile in a 'state of the union' address is itself surprising, and that a head of government should go out of his way to influence a television sitcom is probably unprecedented in the history of language planning! But it well illustrates the direction in which matters are moving. Singlish must now be a significant presence in Singapore for it to attract this level of attention and condemnation. And the nature of the reaction also well illustrates the nature of the problem which all New Englishes encounter, in their early stages. It is the same problem that older varieties of English also encountered: the view that there can only be one kind of English, the standard kind, and that all others should be eliminated. From the days when this mindset first became dominant, in the eighteenth century, Britain and a few other countries have taken some 250 years to confront it and replace it with a more egalitarian perspective in educational curricula. The contemporary view, as represented in the UK National Curriculum, is to maintain the importance of Standard English while at the same time maintaining the value of local accents and dialects. The intellectual basis for this policy is the recognition of the fact that language has many functions, and that the reason for the existence of Standard English (to promote mutual intelligibility) is different from the reason for the

---

[59] For example, *The Straits Times*, 23 August 1999; *Independent*, 17 October 1999.

existence of local dialects (to promote local identity). The same arguments apply, with even greater force, on a global scale. There is no intrinsic conflict between Standard English and Singlish in Singapore, as the reasons for the existence of the former, to permit Singaporeans of different linguistic backgrounds to communicate with each other and with people abroad, are different from the reasons for the emergence of the latter, to provide a sense of local identity. Ironically, the prime minister himself recognized the importance of both these goals, in emphasizing that the future of Singapore needed an outward-looking set of economic and cultural goals as well as an inward-looking sense of the 'something special and precious' in the Singaporean way of life. A bidialectal (or bilingual) policy allows a people to look both ways at once, and would be the most efficient way of the country achieving its aims. Fostering Standard English is one plank of such a policy. Condemning Singlish is not.

Similar attitudes will be encountered in all parts of the world where English is developing a strong non-native presence, and at all levels. Teachers of English as a Second or Foreign Language have to deal with the situation routinely, with students increasingly arriving in the classroom speaking a dialect which is markedly different from Standard English. The question of just how much local phonology, grammar, vocabulary and pragmatics should be allowed in is difficult and contentious. But there seems no doubt that, gradually, there is a definite ameliorative trend around the English-speaking world, with expressions which were once heavily penalized as local and low-class now achieving a degree of status. How fast this trend develops depends on economic and social factors more than on anything else. If the people who use mixed varieties as markers of their identity become more influential, attitudes will change, and usages will become more acceptable. In fifty years' time, we could find ourselves with an English language which contains within itself large areas of contact-influenced vocabulary, borrowed from such languages as Malay or Chinese, being actively used in Singapore, Malaysia and emigrant communities elsewhere. First-language speakers from those areas would instinctively select this vocabulary as their first choice in conversation. Everyone else would recognize their words as legitimate options – passively, at least, with occasional forays into active use. It is a familiar story, in the history of the English language, though operating now on a global scale.

Indeed, such a scenario would not be so different from that already found in English. There are over 350 living languages given as vocabulary sources in the files of the *Oxford English dictionary*. And, for example, there are already over 250 words with Malay as part of their etymology in the *OED*. So the foundation is already laid. The contact-language words of the future will of course include more alternative rather than supplementary expressions – localized words for everyday notions, such as tables and chairs, rather than for regionally restricted notions, such as fauna and flora – but the notion of a lexical mosaic as such is not new. It has always been part of the language.

An English family of languages?

The future of world English is likely to be one of increasing multidialectism; but could this become multilingualism? Is English going to fragment into mutually unintelligible varieties, just as Vulgar Latin did a millennium ago? The forces of the past fifty years, which have led to so many New Englishes, suggest this outcome. If such significant change can be noticed within a relatively short period of time, must not these varieties become even more differentiated over the next century, so that we end up, as McArthur argues, with an English 'family of languages'?[60]

Prophets have been predicting such an outcome for some time. In 1877, the British philologist Henry Sweet (the probable model for Shaw's Henry Higgins in *Pygmalion/My Fair Lady*) thought that a century later 'England, America, and Australia will be speaking mutually unintelligible languages, owing to their independent changes of pronunciation'.[61] The same point had been made nearly a century before by Noah Webster, in his *Dissertations* (1789). Webster thought that such a development would be 'necessary and unavoidable', and would result in 'a language in North America, as different from the future language of England,

[60] McArthur (1998).   [61] Sweet (1877: 196).

as the modern Dutch, Danish and Swedish are from the German, or from one another'.[62] From Webster's pro-American point of view, of course, that would not have been such a bad thing.

Neither of these scholars proved to be accurate prophets. And indeed, it is plain that the question of fragmentation does not have a single simple answer. The history of language suggests that such a course of events has been a frequent phenomenon (as in the well-known case of Latin); but the history of language is no longer a guide. Today, we live in the proverbial global village, where we have immediate access to other languages and varieties of English in ways that have come to be available but recently; and this is having a strong centripetal effect. With a whole range of fresh auditory models becoming routinely available, chiefly through satellite television, it is easy to see how any New English could move in different directions at the same time. The pull imposed by the need for identity, which has been making New Englishes increasingly dissimilar from British English, could be balanced by a pull imposed by the need for intelligibility, on a world scale, which will make them increasingly similar, through the continued use of Standard English. At the former level, there may well be increasing mutual unintelligibility; but at the latter level, there would not.

None of this disallows the possible emergence of a family of English languages in a sociolinguistic sense; but mutual unintelligibility will not be the basis of such a notion in the case of New Englishes, any more than it has been in relation to intranational accents and dialects. Although there are several well-known instances of dialect unintelligibility among people from different regional backgrounds, especially when encountered at rapid conversational speed – in Britain, Cockney (London), Geordie (Newcastle), Scouse (Liverpool) and Glaswegian (Glasgow) are among the most commonly cited cases – the problems largely resolve when a speaker slows down, or they reduce to difficulties over isolated lexical items. This makes regional varieties of English no more problematic for linguistic theory than, say, occupational varieties such as legal or scientific. It is no more illuminating to call

[62] Webster (1789: 23).

Cockney or Scouse 'different English languages' than it would be to call Legal or Scientific by such a name, and anyone who chooses to extend the application of the term 'language' in this way finds a slippery slope which eventually leads to the blurring of the potentially useful distinctions between 'language', 'variety' and 'dialect'.

The intelligibility criterion has traditionally provided little support for an English 'language family'. But we have learned from sociolinguistics in recent decades that this criterion is by no means an adequate explanation for the language nomenclature of the world, as it leaves out of consideration linguistic attitudes, and in particular the criterion of identity. It is this which allows us to say that people from Norway, Sweden and Denmark speak different languages, notwithstanding the considerable amount of intelligibility which exists between them. It seems that if a community wishes its way of speaking to be considered a 'language', and if they have the political power to support their decision, there is nothing which can stop them doing so. The present-day ethos is to allow communities to deal with their own internal policies themselves, as long as these are not perceived as being a threat to others. However, to promote an autonomous language policy, two criteria need to be satisfied. The first is to have a community with a single mind about the matter, and the second is to have a community which has enough political–economic 'clout' to make its decision be respected by outsiders with whom it is in regular contact. When these criteria are lacking, any such movement is doomed.

There are very few examples of English generating varieties which are given totally different names, and even fewer where these names are rated as 'languages' (as opposed to 'dialects'). There are some cases among the English-derived pidgins and creoles around the world (e.g. *Tok Pisin, Gullah*), but any proposal for language status is invariably surrounded with controversy. An instance from the mid-1990s is the case of *Ebonics* – a blend of Ebony + phonics – proposed for the variety of English spoken by African Americans, and which had previously been called by such names as *Black Vernacular English* or *African-American Vernacular English*.[63] Although the intentions behind the proposal were

---

[63] Perry and Delpit (1998).

noble, and attracted some support, it was denounced by people from across the political and ethnic spectrum, including such prominent individuals as Education Secretary Richard W. Riley, the black civil rights leader Revd Jesse Jackson, and writer Maya Angelou. Quite evidently the two criteria above did not obtain: the US black community did not have a single mind about the matter, and the people who had the political–economic clout to make the decision be respected also had mixed views about it.

By giving a distinct name, Ebonics, to what had previously been recognized as a variety of English, a hidden boundary in the collective unconscious seems to have been crossed. It is in fact very unusual to assign a novel name to a variety of English in this way, other than in the humorous literature, where such names as *Strine* (a spelling of an imagined casual Australian pronunciation of the word 'Australian') can be found. There are indeed many world English locations which have generated their regional humour book, in which the local accent or dialect is illustrated by comic 'translations' into Standard English.[64] Exchanges of this kind, however, are part of the genre of language play, and recognized as such by author and reader. They are not serious attempts to upgrade the status of the dialect into a separate language. The notion of translation which they employ is purely figurative. Indeed, the humour depends on a tacit recognition of the fact that we are dealing with a variety which is 'non-standard', and that people can recognize what it is saying. There is no true intelligibility problem and no problem of identity status.

There is one clear case where a specific regional variety of English has acquired a new name as part of its claim to be recognized as a standard in its locality: Scots. Here is McArthur's summary of the situation:[65]

The people of Scotland occupy a unique historical and cultural position in the English-speaking world. They use the standard language (with distinctive phonological, grammatical, lexical, and idiomatic features) in administration, law, education, the media, all national institutions, and

[64] See Crystal (1998: 18–24) on regional dialect play.
[65] McArthur (1998: 138), here and below.

by and large in their dealings with Anglophones elsewhere, but in their everyday lives a majority of them mix 'the King's English' with what in an earlier age was called 'the King's Scots'.

How does Scots stand in relation to the two criteria referred to above? The situation is complex, because the Scots community does not have a single mind about the matter, nor has it had enough political–economic power to make any decision be respected by outsiders. In relation to the former point, the case in favour has been strongly argued by the leading scholar on Scots, Jack Aitken. After reviewing the arguments, he concludes:[66]

All the phenomena just recounted – the distinctiveness of Scots, its still substantial presence in daily speech, the fact that it was once the national language, its identifiably distinct history, its adoption (some Gaels would call it usurpation) of the nation's name, and the massive and remarkable and still vital literature in it, mutually support one another and one further and remarkable phenomenon – the ancient and still persistent notion that Scots is indeed 'the Scottish language'.

But the missionary tone of this quotation, along with the indication that at least one section of the Scottish community thinks differently, suggests a complex sociolinguistic situation; and at the end of his article even Aitken pulls back from the brink: 'I believe what I have written suggests that if Scots is not now a full "language" it is something more than a mere "dialect". A distinguished German scholar once called it a *Halbsprache* – a semi-language.' In relation to the second criterion, it remains to be seen whether the changing political situation in Scotland (the 1997 referendum on devolution agreeing the formation of a new Scots Assembly) will produce a stronger voice in favour of Scots. McArthur is doubtful: 'Any political change in the condition of Scotland is unlikely to have a direct influence on the shaky condition of Scots or Gaelic, because the movement for Scottish autonomy (within the EU) does not have a linguistic dimension to it.' If he is right, then that eliminates the strongest traditional contender for a separate identity within an English family of languages.

[66] Aitken (1985: 44).

In all these cases of emerging linguistic status, however, the number of speakers involved has been a minority, within a much larger sociopolitical entity. We have yet to see whether the same situation will obtain in countries where the New English speakers are in a majority and hold political power, or in locations where new, supranational political relationships are being formed. For example, although several languages are co-official in the European Union, pragmatic linguistic realities result in English being the most widely used language in these corridors (see p. 12). But what kind of common English emerges, when Germans, French, Greeks and others come into contact, each using English with its own pattern of interference from the mother tongue? There will be the usual sociolinguistic accommodation,[67] and the result will be a novel variety, of 'Euro-English' – a term which has been used for over a decade with reference to the distinctive vocabulary of the Union (with its *Eurofighters*, *Eurodollars*, *Eurosceptics* and so on), but which must now be extended to include the various hybrid accents, grammatical constructions and discourse patterns encountered there. On several occasions, I have encountered English-as-a-first-language politicians, diplomats and civil servants working in Brussels commenting on how they have felt their own English being pulled in the direction of these foreign-language patterns. A common feature, evidently, is to accommodate to an increasingly syllable-timed rhythm. Others include the use of simplified sentence constructions, the avoidance of idioms and colloquial vocabulary, a slower rate of speech, and the use of clearer patterns of articulation (avoiding some of the assimilations and elisions which would be natural in a first-language setting). It is important to stress that this is not the 'foreigner talk' reported in an earlier ELT era. These people are not 'talking down' to their colleagues, or consciously adopting simpler expressions, for the English of their interlocutors may be as fluent as their own. It is a natural process of accommodation, which in due course could lead to new standardized forms.

It is plain that the emergence of hybrid trends and varieties raises all kinds of theoretical and pedagogical questions, several of

---

[67] Giles and Smith (1979).

which began to be addressed during the 1990s.[68] They blur the long-standing distinctions between 'first', 'second' and 'foreign' language. They make us reconsider the notion of 'standard', especially when we find such hybrids being used confidently and fluently by groups of people who have education and influence in their own regional setting. They present the traditionally clear-cut notion of 'translation' with all kinds of fresh problems, for (to go back to the Malaysian example) at what point in a conversation should we say that a notion of translation is relevant, as we move from 'understanding' to 'understanding most of the utterance precisely' to 'understanding little of the utterance precisely ("getting the drift" or "gist")' to 'understanding none of the utterance, despite its containing several features of English'? And, to move into the sociolinguistic dimension, hybrids give us new challenges in relation to language attitudes: for example, at what point would our insistence on the need for translation cause an adverse reaction from the participants, who might maintain they are 'speaking English', even though we cannot understand them?

This whole topic is so recent that it is difficult to make predictions with much confidence. Many of the new varieties have grown extremely rapidly, so that it is difficult to establish their role in their society, or how people are reacting to them. In several cases, it is known that the rise of a local English generates controversy within the community. Some writers seize on the new variety with enthusiasm, and try to make it even more distinctive. Others prefer to retain strong links with the British or American standard. Some teachers, likewise, allow the new forms into their teaching; others rule them out.

The Indian author Raja Rao, writing in 1963, was one who looked forward to the development of a new Indian English:[69]

English is not really an alien language to us. It is the language of our intellectual make-up – like Sanskrit and Persian was before – but not of our emotional make-up . . . We cannot write like the English. We should not. We cannot write only as Indians. We have grown to look at the large world as part of us. Our method of expression has to be a dialect which

---

[68] See the range of issues addressed in Schneider (1997) and Foley (1999).
[69] Rao (1963: vii).

will some day prove to be as distinctive and colourful as the Irish or the American.

And a similar view comes from Salman Rushdie, in the essay referred to:

I don't think it is always necessary to take up the anti-colonial – or is it post-colonial? – cudgels against English. What seems to me to be happening is that those peoples who were once colonized by the language are now rapidly remaking it, domesticating it, becoming more and more relaxed about the way they use it. Assisted by the English language's enormous flexibility and size, they are carving out large territories for themselves within its front.

To take the case of India, only because it's the one in which I'm most familiar. The debate about the appropriateness of English in post-British India has been raging ever since 1947; but today, I find, it is a debate which has meaning only for the older generation. The children of independent India seem not to think of English as being irredeemably tainted by its colonial provenance. They use it as an Indian language, as one of the tools they have to hand.

The Nigerian novelist Chinua Achebe has made one of the clearest statements representing the middle-of-the-road position:[70]

The price a world language must be prepared to pay is submission to many different kinds of use. The African writer should aim to use English in a way that brings out his message best without altering the language to the extent that its value as a medium of international exchange will be lost. He should aim at fashioning out an English which is at once universal and able to carry his peculiar experience . . . I feel that English will be able to carry the weight of my African experience. But it will have to be a new English, still in full communion with its ancestral home but altered to suit its new African surroundings.

In the years since these remarks were made, this is precisely what has been happening – and not only in Africa, but throughout the countries of the outer circle. There is even a suggestion that some of the territories of the expanding circle – those in which English is learned as a foreign language – may be bending English to suit

[70] Achebe (1964: 62).

their purposes, as in the case of Euro-English (p. 182). Local usages are emerging, and achieving standard status within a region. For example, 'Welcome in Egypt' is now so established among Egyptian speakers of English, of all educational backgrounds and social classes, that it must now be seen as a variant as standard in character as is the prepositional variation between 'quarter to' and 'quarter of' in US and UK time-telling.[71]

If Englishes did become increasingly different, as years went by, the consequences for world English would not necessarily be fatal. A likely scenario is that our current ability to use more than one dialect would simply extend to meet the fresh demands of the international situation. A new form of English – let us think of it as 'World Standard Spoken English' (WSSE) – would almost certainly arise. Indeed, the foundation for such a development is already being laid around us.

Most people are already 'multidialectal' to a greater or lesser extent. They use one spoken dialect at home, when they are with their family or talking to other members of their local community: this tends to be an informal variety, full of casual pronunciation, colloquial grammar, and local turns of phrase. They use another spoken dialect when they are away from home, travelling to different parts of their country or interacting with others at their place of work: this tends to be a formal variety, full of careful pronunciation, conventional grammar, and standard vocabulary. Those who are literate have learned a third variety, that of written standard English which (apart from a few minor differences, such as British vs. American spelling) currently unites the English-speaking world.

In a future where there were many national Englishes, little would change. People would still have their dialects for use within their own country, but when the need came to communicate with people from other countries they would slip into WSSE. So, a multinational company might decide to hold a conference at which representatives from each of its country operations would be present. The reps from Kolkata, sharing a cab on their way to

[71] It has begun to be cited as accepted usage in some local editions of ELT textbooks.

the conference, would be conversing in informal Indian English. The reps from Lagos, in their cab, would be talking in informal Nigerian English. The reps from Los Angeles would be using informal American English. Any one of these groups, overhearing any other, might well find the conversation difficult to follow. But when all meet at the conference table, there would be no problem: everyone would be using WSSE.

People who attend international conferences, or who write scripts for an international audience, or who are 'talking' on the Internet have probably already felt the pull of this new variety. It takes the form, for example, of consciously avoiding a word or phrase which you know is not going to be understood outside your own country, and of finding an alternative form of expression. It can also affect your pronunciation and grammar. But it is too early to be definite about the way this variety will develop. WSSE is still in its infancy. Indeed, it has hardly yet been born.

If one happens to be in the right place at the right time, one can glimpse the birth pangs. I saw such a pang while attending an international seminar at a European university in the late 1990s. Around the table were representatives of some twenty countries. There were two people from the UK, two from the USA, and one from Australia, with the others all from countries where English was either a second (official) language or a foreign language. The lingua franca of the meeting was English, and everyone seemed to be using the language competently – even the native speakers. We were well into the discussion period following a paper which had generated a lively buzz of comment and counter-comment. Someone then made a telling remark. There was a silence round the table, which was broken by one of the US delegates observing: 'That came from out in left field.' There was another silence, and I could see some of the delegates turning to their neighbours in a surreptitious way, as one does when one does not understand what on earth is going on, and wants to check that one is not alone. But they were not pondering the telling remark. They were asking each other what 'from out in left field' meant. My neighbour asked me: as a native speaker, he felt confident I would know. I did not know. Baseball at that time was a closed book to me – and still is, very largely.

One of the braver of the delegates spoke up: 'Out where?', he asked. It took the US delegate by surprise, as plainly he had never had that idiom questioned before; but he managed to explain that it was a figure of speech from baseball, a ball coming from an unusual direction, and what he had meant was that the remark was surprising, unexpected. There were nods of relief from around the table. Then one of the UK delegates chipped in: 'You played that with a straight bat', he said. 'Huh?', said the American. 'Oh, I say, that's not cricket', I added, parodically. 'Isn't it?', asked a delegate from Asia, now totally confused. The next few minutes of the meeting were somewhat chaotic. The original theme was quite forgotten, as people energetically debated the meaning of cricket and baseball idioms with their neighbours. Those who could added their own local version of how they said things like that in their part of the world – the sports metaphors they lived by. Eventually, the chairman called everyone back to order, and the discussion of the paper continued. But my attention was blown, and I spent the remainder of the session listening not to what delegates were saying, but to how they were saying it.

What was immediately noticeable was that the native speakers seemed to become much less colloquial. In particular, I did not sense any further use of national idioms. Indeed, the speakers seemed to be going out of their way to avoid them. I made a small contribution towards the end, and I remember thinking while I was doing it – 'don't use any cricket terms'. Afterwards, in the bar, others admitted to doing the same. My British colleague said he had consciously avoided using the word *fortnight*, replacing it by *two weeks*. And, as the evening wore on, people began apologizing facetiously when they noticed themselves using a national idiom, or when somebody else used one. It became something of a game – the kind that linguists love to play. There was one nice moment when the US, UK and Australian delegates were all reduced to incoherence because they found that they had disbarred themselves from using any of their natural expressions for 'the safe walking route at the side of a road' – *pavement* (UK), *sidewalk* (US) and *footpath* (Australian). In the absence of a regionally neutral term, all they were left with was circumlocution (such as the one just given).

It is only an anecdote, but it is an intriguing one, as it illustrates one of the directions in which people can go as they move towards a WSSE. It did not have to be that direction. It would have been perfectly possible for the seminar group to have gone down another road: to have adopted 'out in left field' as an idiom, everyone adding it to their own idiolect – de-Americanizing it, as it were. That did not happen, on that occasion, though it seems to be happening a lot elsewhere. US English does seem likely to be the most influential in the development of WSSE. The direction of influence has for some time been largely one-way. Many grammatical issues in contemporary British usage show the influence of US forms, US spellings are increasingly widespread (especially in computer contexts), and there is a greater passive awareness of distinctively US lexicon in the UK (because of media influence) than vice versa. On the other hand, the situation will be complicated by the emergence on the world scene of new linguistic features derived from the L2 varieties, which as we have seen will in due course become numerically dominant. No feature of L2 English has yet become a part of standard US or UK English; but, as the balance of speakers changes, there is no reason for L2 features not to become part of WSSE. This would be especially likely if there were features which were shared by several (or all) L2 varieties – such as the use of syllable-timed rhythm, or the widespread difficulty observed in the use of *th* sounds.

The development of WSSE can be predicted because it enables people, yet again, to 'have their cake and eat it'. The concept of WSSE does not replace a national dialect: it supplements it. People who can use both are in a much more powerful position than people who can use only one. They have a dialect in which they can continue to express their national identity; and they have a dialect which can guarantee international intelligibility, when they need it. The same dual tendencies can be seen on the Internet, incidentally, which simultaneously presents us with a range of informal identifying personal varieties and a corpus of universally intelligible standard English. It is an interesting context for those wishing to study the forces affecting language change, with users searching for a balance between the attraction of a 'cool', idiosyncratic, but often unintelligible linguistic persona and the need to use an 'uncool' standardized form of expression in order to make oneself understood!

'Having your cake and eating it', of course, also applies to the use of completely different languages as markers of identity. It may well be that the people travelling by cab to the international conference would be speaking Hindi, Hausa, and Spanish, respectively. When they all meet at the conference table, they would switch into WSSE. They do not have to give up their national linguistic identities just because they are going to an international meeting. But of course this scenario assumes that Hindi, Hausa, and Spanish are still respected, alive and well, and living in their respective home communities.

There is nothing unusual, in linguistic terms, about a community using more than one variety (or language) as alternative standards for different purposes. The situation is the familiar one of *diglossia*, as illustrated by the 'high' and 'low' varieties found in such languages as Greek, German and Arabic.[72] It would seem that English at the global level is steadily moving towards becoming a diglossic language. Already, in such locations as Singapore, we see two spoken varieties co-existing (albeit uncomfortably, p. 174), one being used for intelligibility (Standard British English) and the other for identity (Singlish). A similar scenario is found in the Philippines, where Standard American English co-exists alongside Taglish. If WSSE emerges as a neutral global variety in due course, it will make redundant the British/American distinction. British and American English will still exist, of course, but as varieties expressing national identity in the UK and USA. For global purposes, WSSE will suffice.

A unique event?

There has never been a language so widely spread or spoken by so many people as English. There are therefore no precedents to help us see what happens to a language when it achieves genuine world status; and predictions about the future, as we saw in the remarks

[72] Ferguson (1959).

of Noah Webster and Henry Sweet, have a habit of being wrong. The balance between the competing demands of intelligibility and identity is especially fragile, and can easily be affected by social change, such as a swing in immigrant policy, new political alliances, or a change in a country's population trends.

The emergence of English with a genuine global presence therefore has a significance which goes well beyond this particular language. Because there are no precedents for languages achieving this level of use (if we exclude Latin, which was in a sense 'global' when the world was much smaller), we do not know what happens to them in such circumstances. The investigation of world English therefore provides a fresh testing-ground for sociolinguistic hypotheses which previously had only regional validity, and a domain where we may encounter new kinds of phenomena which might one day motivate a global reconceptualization of that subject. What happens to a language when it is spoken by many times more people as a second or foreign language than as a mother-tongue? If English does one day go the same way as Latin and French, and have less of a global role, the next languages to rise (the potential of Spanish, Chinese, Arabic and Hindi/Urdu is highlighted by Graddol (1998: 59)) will doubtless be subject to the same governing factors. So far, although we have a general sense of what these factors are, we have very little understanding of how they interact, and of what happens to the structural character of a language when it achieves a global presence.

If we cannot predict the future, we can at least speculate, and there are some fascinating speculations to be made. It may well be the case, as was intimated earlier, that the English language has already grown to be independent of any form of social control. There may be a critical number or critical distribution of speakers (analogous to the notion of critical mass in nuclear physics) beyond which it proves impossible for any single group or alliance to stop its growth, or even influence its future. If there were to be a major social change in Britain which affected the use of English there, would this have any real effect on the world trend? It is unlikely. And, as we have seen, even the current chief player, the USA, will have decreasing influence as the years go by, because of the way world population is growing.

In 500 years' time, will it be the case that everyone will automatically be introduced to English as soon as they are born (or, by then, very likely, as soon as they are conceived)? If this is part of a rich multilingual experience for our future newborns, this can only be a good thing. If it is by then the only language left to be learned, it will have been the greatest intellectual disaster that the planet has ever known.

If there is a critical mass, does this mean that the emergence of a global language is a unique event, in evolutionary terms? It may be that English, in some shape or form, will find itself in the service of the world community for ever.

References

Achebe, Chinua. 1964. *Morning yet on Creation Day*. London: Heinemann.

Adams, Douglas. 1979. *The hitch-hiker's guide to the galaxy*. London: Pan.

Adams, John. 1780. Letter to the President of Congress (5 September 1780). In C. F. Adams, *The works of John Adams*. Boston: Little, Brown, 1852.

Ahulu, Samuel. 1994. Styles of Standard English. *English Today* 40, 10–16.

    1995a. Variation in the use of complex verbs in international English. *English Today* 42, 28–34.

    1995b. Hybridized English in Ghana. *English Today* 44, 31–6.

    1998a. Lexical variation in international English. *English Today* 55, 29–34.

    1998b. Grammatical variation in international English. *English Today* 56, 19–25.

Aitken, A. J. 1985. Is Scots a language? *English Today* 3, 41–5.

Allsopp, Richard. 1996. *Dictionary of Caribbean English Usage*. Oxford: Oxford University Press.

Alsagoff, Lubna, Bao, Zhiming and Wee, Lionel. 1998. *Why you talk like that?* The pragmatics of a *why* construction in Singapore English. *English World-Wide* 19, 247–60.

Anonymous [Joe Klein]. 1996. *Primary colors*. New York: Random House.

References

Avis, Walter S., Crate, Charles, Drysdale, Patrick, Leechman, Douglas and Scargill, M. H. 1967. *A dictionary of Canadianisms on historical principles*. Toronto: Gage.

Awonusi, Victor O. 1990. Coming of age: English in Nigeria. *English Today* 22, 31–5.

Bailey, Richard W. 1991. *Images of English: a cultural history of the language*. Cambridge: Cambridge University Press.

Baker, Colin and Prys Jones, Sylvia. 1998. *Encyclopedia of bilingualism and bilingual education*. Clevedon: Multilingual Matters.

Bamgbose, Ayo. Ed. 2000. *Sociolinguistics in West Africa*. Berlin: Mouton de Gruyter.

Bamiro, Edmund O. 1994. Innovation in Nigerian English. *English Today* 39, 13–15.

Bansal, R. K. 1990. The pronunciation of English in India. In S. Ramsaran (ed.), *Studies in the pronunciation of English*. London: Routledge, 219–30.

Baskaran, Loga. 1994. The Malaysian English mosaic. *English Today* 37, 27–32.

Bauer, Laurie. 1983. *English word formation*. Cambridge: Cambridge University Press.

1994. English in New Zealand. In Burchfield (1994), 382–429.

Baumgardner, Robert J. 1990. The indigenization of English in Pakistan. *English Today* 21, 59–65.

Ed. 1993. *The English language in Pakistan*. Karachi: Oxford University Press.

1998. Word-formation in Pakistani English. *English World-Wide* 19 (2), 205–46.

Bautista, Maria Lourdes S. Ed. 1997. *English is an Asian language: the Philippine context*. Sydney: Macquarie Library.

Biber, Douglas, Johansson, Stig, Leech, Geoffrey, Conrad, Susan and Finegan, Edward. 1999. *Longman grammar of spoken and written English*. Harlow: Longman.

Bond, Z. S. and Fokes, J. 1985. Non-native patterns of English syllable timing. *Journal of Phonetics* 13, 407–20.

Branford, Jean and Branford, William. 1978/91. *A dictionary of South African English*. Cape Town: Oxford University Press.

Brazil, David. 1995. *A grammar of speech*. Oxford: Oxford University Press.

Brenzinger, Matthias. Ed. 1998. *Endangered languages in Africa*. Cologne: Rüdiger Köper.

Bright, William. Ed. 1992. *International encyclopedia of linguistics*. Oxford: Oxford University Press.

British Council. 1995. English in the world: the English 2000 global consultation. London: The British Council.

1997. *English language teaching*. London: The British Council.

Burchfield, Robert. Ed. 1994. *Cambridge history of the English language*, Vol. V. *English in Britain and overseas*. Cambridge: Cambridge University Press.

Burridge, Kate and Mulder, Jean. 1998. *English in Australia and New Zealand: an introduction to its history, structure and use*. Oxford: Oxford University Press.

Business Week. 1996. A World Wide Web for tout le monde. *Business Week*, 1 April 1996.

Byford, Mark. 2001. BBC World Service: annual review 2000–1. London: BBC.

Cassidy, F. G. 1982. Geographical variation of English in the United States. In Richard W. Bailey and Manfred Görlach (eds.), *English as a world language*. Cambridge: Cambridge University Press, 177–209.

Cassidy, F. G. and Le Page, R. B. Eds. 1967. *Dictionary of Jamaican English*. Cambridge: Cambridge University Press.

Chesterfield, Lord [Philip Dormer Stanhope]. 1754. Letter to *The World*, 28 November 1754.

CILT [Centre for Information on Language Teaching and Research] 2002. *Speaking up for languages*. London: CILT.

Civil Aviation Authority. 2002. *Radiotelephony manual*, 12th edn. London: Civil Aviation Authority.

Columbia encyclopedia, The. 1993. New York: Columbia University Press.

Commission on Global Governance. 1995. Ingvar Carlsson and Sridath Ramphal (co-chairmen), *Our global neighbourhood*. New York: United Nations.

Coulmas, Florian. 1992. *Language and economy*. Oxford: Blackwell.

Crisell, Andrew. 2002. *An introductory history of British broadcasting*, 2nd edn. London: Routledge.

Crystal, David. 1969. *Prosodic systems and intonation in English*. Cambridge: Cambridge University Press.

1995a. *The Cambridge encyclopedia of the English language*. Cambridge: Cambridge University Press.

1995b. Documenting rhythmical change. In J. Windsor-Lewis (ed.), *Studies in general and English phonetics*. London: Routledge, 174–9.

1996. The past, present and future of English rhythm. In M. Vaughan-Rees (ed.), *Changes in pronunciation*, Newsletter of the IATEFL Pronunciation Special Interest Group. Whitstable: International Association of Teachers of English as a Foreign Language, 8–13.

1998. *Language play*. Harmondsworth: Penguin.

1999/2000. On trying to be crystal-clear: a response to Phillipson. *European English Messenger* 8 (1), 1999, 59–65; expanded in *Applied Linguistics* 21, 2000, 415–23.

2000. *Language death*. Cambridge: Cambridge University Press.

2001. *Language and the Internet*. Cambridge: Cambridge University Press.

Dako, Kari. 2001. Ghanaisms: towards a semantic and a formal classification. *English World-Wide* 22 (1), 23–53.

Dalby, Andrew. 2002. Language in danger. Harmondsworth: Penguin.

De Houwer, Annick. 1995. Bilingual language acquisition. In Paul Fletcher and Brian MacWhinney (eds.), *The handbook of child language*. Oxford: Blackwell, 219–50.

Deterding, D. 1994. The intonation of Singapore English. *Journal of the International Phonetic Association* 24, 61–72.

Dickens, Charles. 1842/68. *American notes*. London: Hazell, Watson and Viney.

Dillon, Nancy. 1999. Web should prepare for a non-English majority. *Computerworld*, 14 June.

Dunstan, E. Ed. 1969. *Twelve Nigerian languages*. London: Longmans Green.

Dyja, Eddie. Ed. 2001. *BFI film and television handbook: 2002*. London: British Film Institute.

Eco, Umberto. 1995. *The search for the perfect language*. Oxford: Blackwell.

Elliott, Blanche B. 1962. *A history of English advertising*. London: Business Books.

Encyclopaedia Britannica. 1986. Publishing. *Macropaedia*, Vol. XXVI. Chicago: Encyclopaedia Britannica, 457–92.

2002. *Britannica Book of the Year*. Chicago: Encyclopaedia Britannica.

Ethnologue. 1988, 1992. *Ethnologue: the languages of the world*. 11th, 12th, 13th edns. Dallas: Summer Institute of Linguistics.

European Commission. 2002a. *European Year of Languages 2001: some highlights*. Brussels: European Commission, Language Policy Unit.

2002b. Languages in Europe. http://europa.eu.int/comm/education/languages/lang/europeanlanguages.html

Evans, Stephen and Green, Christopher. 2001. Language in post-colonial Hong Kong: the roles of English and Chinese in the public and private sectors. *English World-Wide* 22, 247–68.

Ferguson, Charles. 1959. Diglossia. *Word*, 15, 325–40.

Fisher, A. E. C. 2000. Assessing the state of Ugandan English. *English Today* 61, 57–61.

Fishman, Joshua A., Conrad, Andrew and Rubal-Lopez, Alma. Eds. 1996. *Post-imperial English*. Berlin and New York: Mouton de Gruyter.

Foley, James A. Ed. 1999. *English in new cultural contexts*. New York: Oxford University Press.

Gandhi, Mohandas K. 1958. *Evil wrought by the English medium*. Ahmedabad: Navajivan.

Giles, H. and Smith, P. 1979. Accommodation theory: optimal levels of convergence. In H. Giles and R. St Clair (eds.), *Language and social psychology*. Oxford: Blackwell, 45–65.

Goh, Christine. 1998. The level tone in Singapore English. *English Today* 53, 50–3.

Gopinathan, Saravanan, Pakir, Anne, Kam, Ho Wah and Saravanan, Vanithamani. Eds. 1998. *Language, society and education in Singapore: issues and trends*, 2nd edn. Singapore: Times Academic Press.

Görlach, Manfred. 1995. Dictionaries of transplanted Englishes. In Manfred Görlach, *More Englishes: new studies in varieties of English 1988–1994*. Amsterdam: Benjamins, 124–63.

1996. And is it English? *English World-Wide*, 17 (2), 153–74.

2002. Ed. *English in Europe*. Oxford: Oxford University Press.

Goundry, Norman. 2001. Why Unicode won't work on the Internet: linguistic, political and technical limitations. http://www.hastingsresearch.com/net/04-unicode-limitations.shtml

Graddol, David. 1998. *The future of English*. London: The British Council.

1999. The decline of the native speaker. In David Graddol and Ulrike H. Meinhof (eds.), *English in a changing world. AILA Review* 13, 57–68.

Grant Thornton. 2002. *European business survey*. London: Grant Thornton.

Grimm, Jakob. 1851. Über den Ursprung der Sprache. *Kleineren Schrifte* 1, 1965, 255–98.

Gronow, Pekka, Saunio, Ilpo and Moseley, Christopher. 1998. *An international history of the recording industry*. London: Continuum.

References

Gyasi, Ibrahim K. 1991. Aspects of English in Ghana. *English Today* 26, 26–31.

Harrison, Deborah Sears and Trabasso, Tom. Eds. 1976. *Black English: a seminar*. Hillsdale: Erlbaum.

Herriman, Michael and Burnaby, Barbara. Eds. 1996. *Language policies in English-dominant countries*. Clevedon: Multilingual Matters.

Hughes, Joan. Ed. 1989. *The concise Australian national dictionary*. Melbourne: Oxford University Press.

Hume, David. 1767. Letter to Edward Gibbon (24 October 1767). In J. Y. T. Greig (ed.), *The letters of David Hume*, Vol. II. Oxford: Clarendon Press, 1932.

Janson, Tore. 2002. *Speak: a short history of languages*. Oxford: Oxford University Press.

Johnson, Edward. 1993. *PoliceSpeak: police communications and language and the Channel Tunnel*. Cambridge: PoliceSpeak Publications.

Jowitt, David. 2000. Patterns of Nigerian English intonation. *English World-Wide* 21 (1), 63–80.

Kachru, Braj. 1985. Institutionalized second-language varieties. In Sidney Greenbaum (ed.), *The English language today*. Oxford: Pergamon, 211–26.

1986. *The alchemy of English*. Oxford: Pergamon.

1988. The sacred cows of English. *English Today* 16, 3–8.

1994. English in South Asia. In Burchfield (1994), 497–553.

2001. World Englishes and culture wars. In T. C. Kiong, A. Pakir, B. K. Choon and R. B. H. Goh (eds.), *Ariels: departures and returns: essays for Edwin Thumboo*. Singapore: Oxford University Press, 392–414.

Kemp, J. A. 1972. *John Wallis's grammar of the English language*. London: Longman.

Lanham, L. W. 1990. Stress and intonation and the intelligibility of South African Black English. In S. Ramsaran (ed.), *Studies in the pronunciation of English*. London: Routledge, 243–60.

Large, Andrew. 1983. *The foreign-language barrier*. London: Deutsch.

Laver, John. 1994. *Principles of phonetics*. Cambridge: Cambridge University Press.

Li, David C. S. 1999. The functions and status of English in Hong Kong: a post-1997 update. *English World-Wide* 20, 67–110.

Linguistic Society of America. 1996. Statement on language rights. In *1995 Annual Report*. Washington: Linguistic Society of America.

Longe, V. U. 1999. Student slang from Benin, Nigeria. *English World-Wide* 20 (2), 237–49.

Lysandrou, Photis and Lysandrou, Yvonne. In press. Global English and proregression: understanding English language spread in the contemporary era. To appear in *Economy and Society*. Paper given to conference on 'The cultural politics of English as a world language', Freiburg, June 2001.

Mashabela, Harry. 1983. Isintu is a self-denial. *Frontline* 3 (8), 17.

McArthur, Tom. 1992. *The Oxford companion to the English language*. Oxford: Oxford University Press.

1998. *The English languages*. Cambridge: Cambridge University Press.

Mehrotra, Raja Ram. 1997. Reduplication in Indian Pidgin English. *English Today* 50, 45–9.

Mencken, H. L. 1945. *The American Language,* Supplement 1. New York: Knopf.

Mesthrie, Rajend. 1992a. *English in language shift*. Cambridge: Cambridge University Press.

1992b. *Lexicon of South African English*. Leeds: Peepal Tree Press.

1993a. English in South Africa. *English Today* 33, 27–33.

1993b. South African Indian English. *English Today* 34, 12–16, 63.

Millar, David, Millar, Ian, Millar, John and Millar, Margaret. Eds. 1989. *Chambers concise dictionary of scientists*. Edinburgh: Chambers.

Mufwene, Salikoko S. 2001. *The ecology of language evolution*. Cambridge: Cambridge University Press.

2002. Colonization, globalization, and the future of languages in the twenty-first century. Translated paper based on a contribution to a UNESCO debate, Paris, September 2001.

Mulcaster, Richard. 1582. *The first part of the Elementarie*. Ed. E. T. Campagnac. Oxford: Clarendon Press, 1925.

Ngũgĩ wa Thiong'o. 1986. *Decolonising the mind*. London: Heinemann/Currey.

Nowell-Smith, Geoffrey. Ed. 1996. *The Oxford history of world cinema*. Oxford: Oxford University Press.

Nunberg, Geoffrey. 1999. Speaking of America: why English-Only is a bad idea. In Rebecca S. Wheeler (ed.), *The workings of language*. Westport: Praeger, 117–28.

2000. Will the Internet always speak English? *American Prospect*, 11 (10), 27 March–10 April.

Orsman, Harry W. 1997. *The dictionary of New Zealand English*. Auckland: Oxford University Press.

Parker, Geoffrey. Ed. 1986. *The world: an illustrated history*. London: Time Books.

References

Pennycook, Alistair. 1994. *The cultural politics of English as an international language*. London: Longman.
　2001. *Critical applied linguistics*. New York: Erlbaum.
Perry, Theresa and Delpit, Lisa. Eds. 1998. *The real Ebonics debate: power, language, and the education of African-American children*. Boston: Beacon.
Phillipson, Robert. 1992. *Linguistic imperialism*. Oxford: Oxford University Press.
　1998/1999. Review of Crystal (1997). *European English Messenger* 7 (2), 1998, 53–6. Expanded in *Applied Linguistics* 20, 1999, 265–76.
Picturegoer Weekly. 1933. *The picturegoer's who's who and encyclopaedia of the screen to-day*. London: Odhams.
Pike, Kenneth L. 1945. *The intonation of American English*. Ann Arbor: University of Michigan Press.
Pitman, Isaac. 1873. English. *The Phonetic Journal* 32 (37), 13 September 1873, 289–90.
Platt, John and Weber, Heidi. 1980. *English in Singapore and Malaysia*. Oxford: Oxford University Press.
Presbrey, F. S. 1929. *The history and development of advertising*. New York: Greenwood.
Preshous, A. 2001. Where you going ah? *English Today* 65, 46–53.
Quirk, Randolph. 1960. The survey of English usage. In *Transactions of the Philological Society*. Reprinted in *Essays on the English language medieval and modern*. London: Longman, 1968, 70–87.
　1962. *The use of English*. London: Longman.
　1985. The English language in a global context. In Randolph Quirk and H. G. Widdowson (eds.), *English in the world*. Cambridge: Cambridge University Press, 1–6.
Quirk, Randolph, Greenbaum, Sydney, Leech, Geoffrey and Svartvik, Jan. 1985. *A comprehensive grammar of the English language*. London: Longman.
Ramphal, Sridath. 1996. World language: opportunities, challenges, responsibilities. Paper given at the World Members' Conference of the English-Speaking Union, Harrogate, UK.
Rao, Raja. 1963. *Kanthapura*. London: Allen and Unwin.
Reynolds, Nick. 1996. Worldwide popular music. *Concord* 3, 9.
Roach, Peter. 1982. On the distinction between 'stress-timed' and 'syllable-timed' languages. In David Crystal (ed.), *Linguistic controversies*. London: Arnold, 73–9.

References

Robinson, David. 1995. The Hollywood conquest. In *Encyclopaedia Britannica Book of the Year*. Chicago: Encyclopaedia Britannica, 245.

Rushdie, Salman. 1991. *Imaginary homelands: essays and criticism 1981–1991*. New York and London: Viking.

Russel, W. P. 1801. *Multum in parvo*. London: Barrett.

Ryan, Keith. Ed. 1999. *The official commemorative album for the millennium*. London: Citroen Wolf Communications.

Said, Halimah Mohd and Siew, Ng Keat. Eds. 2000. *English is an Asian language: the Malaysian context*. Sydney: Macquarie Library.

Schneider, E. W. Ed. 1997. *Englishes around the world*. Amsterdam: Benjamins.

2000. Feature diffusion vs. contact effects in the evolution of New Englishes: a typological case study of negation patterns. *English World-Wide* 21 (2), 201–30.

Serjeantson, Mary. 1935. *A history of foreign words in English*. London: Routledge and Kegan Paul.

Siegel, J. 1995. How to get a laugh in Fijian: code-switching and humour. *Language in Society* 24, 95–110.

Silva, Penny. Ed. 1996. *A dictionary of South African English on historical principles*. Oxford: Oxford University Press.

Skandera, Paul. 1999. What do we *really* know about Kenyan English? A pilot study in research methodology. *English World-Wide* 20 (2), 217–36.

Specter, Michael. 1996. Computer Speak; World, Wide, Web: three English words. *The New York Times*, 14 April 1996, section 4, 1.

Sutcliffe, David. 1982. *British Black English*. Oxford: Blackwell.

Sweet, Henry. 1877. *A handbook of phonetics*. Oxford: Clarendon Press.

Tieken-Boon van Ostade, Ingrid. Ed. 1996. *Two hundred years of Lindley Murray*. Muenster: Nodus Publikationen.

Todd, Loreto. 1984. *Modern Englishes: pidgins and creoles*. Oxford: Blackwell.

Tripathi, P. D. 1990. English in Zambia. *English Today* 23, 34–8.

Union of International Associations. 1996. *Yearbook*, 2nd edn. Brussels: Union of International Associations.

Wallechinsky, David, Wallace, Irving and Wallace, Amy. Eds. 1977. *The book of lists*. London: Cassell.

Wallraff, Barbara. 2000. *What* global language? *Atlantic Monthly*, November, 52–66.

Webster, Noah. 1789. *Dissertations on the English language*. Gainesville: Scholars' Facsimiles and Reprints, 1951.

Weeks, Fred, Glover, Alan, Strevens, Peter and Johnson, Edward. 1984. *Seaspeak reference manual*. Oxford: Pergamon.

Wells, John. 1982. *Accents of English*. Vol. III. *Beyond the British Isles*. Cambridge: Cambridge University Press.

White, William. 1872. Reasons for a phonetic representation of the English language. *The Schoolmaster*, 28 December.

Williamson, Juanita V. and Burke, Virginia M. Eds. 1971. *A various language: perspectives on American dialects*. New York: Holt, Rinehart and Winston.

Winer, Lise. 1989. Trinbagonian. *English Today* 18, 17–22.

Index

The alphabetical arrangement of the index is letter-by-letter.

Index

Babel fish 27
Babel myth 15
Babel site 117
Back to Babel 1
Baekeland, Leo 81
Baez, Joan 103
Bahamas 62
Bahasa Malaysia 57
Bailey, Richard 74, 75
Baker, Colin 17, 90, 137
Balkanization 132
Bamgbose, Ayo 54
Bamiro, Edmund 163
Bandaranaike, Sirimavo 111
Bangladesh 47, 62, 144
banking 83
Bank of English 148
Bansal, R. K. 170
Bao, Zhiming 157
Barbados 62
baseball idiom 186–8
Baskaran, Loga 153–6, 166
Basque 120
Bauer, Laurie 147, 160
Baumgardner, Robert J. 153–5, 160,
    163
Bautista, Maria 57
BBC *see* British Broadcasting
    Corporation
BBC English Radio 97
Beatles, The 102
Bechuanaland 53
begging 104
Belau 56
Belize 62
Bentinck, William 47
Bermuda 62
Bessemer, Henry 81
Bhutan 47
Biber, Douglas 148–52
bidialectism 176
bilingual education 130–40
bilingualism 11–14, 17, 22, 45, 57,
    108–9, 127, 129, 137–8, 176
Billings, Josh 143
biogeography 146
Bismarck 85
Black Vernacular English 179–80
blending 160
Boeing survey 110
Bolton, Whitney 145
Bond, Z. S. 170
borrowings 8, 22–3, 146, 158–62, 166
Bosnian 22

Boston News-Letter 91
Botswana 53, 62
Boulton, Matthew 80
Branford, Jean 159, 161–2
Branford, William 159, 161–2
Brazil 71
Brazil, David 149
Brenzinger, Matthias 24
Bright, William 69
British Broadcasting Corporation (BBC)
    96–8
British Council, The 68, 112–13
British East India Company 47, 56
British Empire *see* United Kingdom,
    colonialism
British English *see* United Kingdom
British Film Institute 99
British Isles 21, 30–1
British National Corpus 148
British Virgin Islands 62
broadcasting xi, 95–8
Brunei 62
Brunel, Marc Isambard 81
Brunswick (records) 101
Burchfield, Robert 147
Burke, Virginia 33
Burnaby, Barbara 36, 39, 41, 46, 129
Burridge, Kate 41
Burton, Richard 52
Burundi 67
business management 16
business surveys 19
Business Week 115
Byford, Mark 97

Cabot, John 36
Cameroon 52, 62, 71, 86
Cameroon Pidgin 52
Canada 21, 36–9, 60, 62, 66, 71, 96,
    127–8, 132, 134, 144
Cannes Film Festival 99
Caribbean 38–40, 99, 119, 144, 171
Cartier, Jacques 36
Cassidy, Frederic G. 143, 161, 162
Cayman Isles 62
Celtic languages 21, 30, 73
censorship 91
Central America 21
Centre for Information on Language
    Teaching 19
Chambers concise dictionary of scientists
    81
Channel Tunnel 107
character sets 116

Index

Index

Index